THE LORD
FOR THE
BODY

THE LORD FOR THE BODY

Discovering God's Plan
for Divine Health and Healing

by

A.B. SIMPSON

234.137

CHRISTIAN PUBLICATIONS
CAMP HILL, PENNSYLVANIA

Christian Publications
3825 Hartzdale Drive, Camp Hill, PA 17011

Faithful, biblical publishing since 1883

ISBN: 0-87509-624-7
LOC Catalog Card Number: 95-70299
© 1996 by Christian Publications
All rights reserved
Printed in the United States of America

96 97 98 99 00 5 4 3 2 1

Cover Design by: Rob Baddorf

CONTENTS

Preface

In 1903 Dr. A.B. Simpson first issued a little volume, under the title of "The Discovery of Divine Healing," in which he set forth the teaching regarding healing as unfolded in different books and in the experiences of various biblical characters. This early volume was not intended to be an exhaustive treatise of this important theme, but was rather a presentation of helpful expositions that centered around the lives of outstanding witnesses to the possibility of supernatural life for the body.

This volume is an enlargement of the early edition. Important chapters upon "Paul and Divine Healing" and "Natural and Supernatural Healing" have been added. Also one of Dr. Simpson's strongest pamphlets on "Inquiries and Answers Concerning Divine Healing" has been included. This contains clear and logical replies to questions that usually arise in the minds of sincere inquirers after the truth. We are confident that this book will prove to be one of the most illuminating and widely appreciated works from the gifted pen of Dr. Simpson.

Because the subject of the Lord's healing is now so widely discussed in Christian circles, it is hard to realize that not many years ago only a few teachers ever touched upon this phase of scriptural doctrine. Probably no one teacher has been so much used of God in this connection as Dr. Simpson. In the minds of multitudes his name is inseparably connected with teaching about divine healing. Yet it is well to remember that Dr. Simpson consistently maintained that he was not the founder of a healing cult, nor did he wish to place healing before spiritual blessing and the salvation of the lost. He preached Christ, the living, all-sufficient Savior. His dominant purpose was to make Him known in all the neglected lands of earth. His heart yearned over the lost and neglected at home and abroad. While faithful to the whole truth of God, he nevertheless placed soul-saving, the instruction of believers in deeper spiritual truths, and earnest missionary efforts before any ministry of healing.

His teaching is best summed up in one of his own poems.

> *Once it was the blessing, Now it is the Lord;*
> *Once it was the feeling, Now it is His Word;*
> *Once His gift I wanted, Now the Giver own;*
> *Once I sought for healing, Now Himself alone.*
> *All in all forever, Jesus will I sing;*
> *Everything in Jesus, And Jesus everything.*

(The complete poem is included in the booklet "Himself" which is available from Christian Publications.)

W. M. Turnbull

Introduction

These delightfully interesting studies come back to us as fresh and winsome as when they first fell from the lips of the honored servant of God, whom many of us held as the Moses who led us through the wilderness of perplexity, the Joshua who inspired us to cross the Jordan into the land of decision.

Some who stood loyally with Dr. Albert Simpson in the early years of his wonderful ministry, like the disciples of old, went away, a few to utter repudiation of the truth they had learned through him. Others held it with cautious reservation. But he lived through all the heartaches which accompanied such departures, sweet and patient, trusting and loving, ever ready to receive them. For he, himself, never varied in the conviction that healing, as he was moved to present it, could not be divorced from the message of salvation. If our blessed Lord is the very life of His own, that life must be related to every department of our being.

With him, the espousal of this much disputed doctrine was not a matter of novelty that would in time wear away and be replaced by other novelties. It gripped his whole being. It compelled his entire devotion. It absorbed his heart and mind. And we who saw the workings of his methods and life must confess that he was moved by a complete surrender to the Holy Spirit. If only he could be found yielding to His behest in every turn he had to take, it was enough. The critics might pierce the atmosphere in which he lived with the arrows of poisoned unbelief; he was immune from infection. He literally was hid in God. It was this that made his messages so sacred to us.

The painful fact that teachers of Christian healing are subtly introducing psychology, that evident antagonist to the Holy Spirit, calls for the highest commendation of his manner. For he never permitted his teaching to be colored with any element of self-effort, self-introspection, self-poise. To him, the truth of healing lay absolutely in the gift of God to His own, by simple acceptance and childlike following in the way of God. Faith unalloyed was his foundation. And the death of self that Christ might live was the super-structure of his teaching and experience.

Those who did not know him personally may well pursue these studies with deep appreciation. For thus they will learn to know the man as well as to accept the truth he held so precious.

Kenneth MacKenzie

CHAPTER 1

The Discovery
of Divine Healing

*And the LORD showed him a piece of wood. He
threw it into the water, and the water became
sweet.*

*There the LORD made a decree and a law for
them, and there he tested them. He said, "If you
listen carefully to the voice of the LORD your God
and do what is right in his eyes, if you pay attention to his commands and keep all his decrees, I
will not bring on you any of the diseases I
brought on the Egyptians, for I am the LORD,
who heals you." (Exodus 15:25-26)*

This was the discovery to Moses of divine healing. The branch that was cast into the bitter
waters had been there before, but undiscovered,
and now the Lord showed it to him and the waters were healed.

A Wonderful Discovery

What a wonderful epoch it marks in our lives
when we discover the hidden promises whose re-

ality and power we had never dreamed of before! Henceforth life becomes all new. How wonderful to find that ever since the Savior died our complete redemption has been purchased. It is only waiting for our faith to claim it. How we wish that all the world might know the treasure it is losing and the hidden resources of help and blessing which lie, like the undiscovered wealth of some secret mine, beneath our thoughtless feet.

The branch that Moses found simply represents the promise of God. Our Bible is full of such promises. All we need is the divine illumination to show them to us, and then the faith to claim them and apply them in the hour of need.

The sweetening of the bitter waters of Marah is closely connected in this passage with the ordinance of healing which God immediately proceeds to give to Israel. It is evident, therefore, that the healing of the waters was intended to suggest the other healing covered by the divine promise. And what a promise it is! It lays the deep and solid foundation of the Lord's supernatural life for all our physical need. What a difference it makes in our lives when we truly find and fully understand this strong and sure foundation for faith to rest upon.

God's Primary School

Notice how early this experience came into the history of ancient Israel. Like a fond mother who first cares for her baby's body and afterwards attends to its education, so God first provides for Israel's physical needs and a little later puts His infant people to school at Mount Sinai and through the deeper lessons of the wilderness. The Lord Jesus began His ministry with physical healing, and so the youngest and humblest child of God ought to know the healing power of the Savior. It is not surprising, therefore, that it comes naturally to our simple-hearted converts in heathen lands, who know no better than to trust the Lord for both body and soul.

Older Than the Law

This ordinance of healing in the 15th chapter of Exodus is much older than the law of Sinai, and, therefore, it has not been superseded even to the passing away of the law. Just as Paul tells the Galatians that the covenant with Abraham could not be annulled by the later law of Moses, so the ordinance of healing stands even after the passing away of the Mosaic institutions. The very terms "decree" and "law" express permanency in this divine provision. And so it stands today, unless we can find in the New Testament some authoritative statement revoking it, which certainly we will not find. For all the teachings of Christ and His apostles are but the echo and the fuller expression of the deep truths so well expressed in this ancient law of healing.

A Test Question

It is announced emphatically in the narrative that this was to be a test question with God's people. There "he tested them" (Exodus 15:25); and what a test it is today of Christian life and Christian faith! How few there are that dare to stand it, and how it proves the people of God! How it brings us up to His heartsearching light and compels us to walk in holy fellowship and obedience if we would find the promises true in our bodies. How rigidly it demands an obedience as deep and spiritual as the profoundest teachings of the New Testament require.

It is not enough that we do our best and sincerely follow the light we have, but we must "listen carefully to the voice of the LORD" (15:26) our God. We must take pains to understand His will. We must have a yielded, willing and responsive conscience that fears to offend and jealously feels its way into all His will. And so, while divine healing is the privilege of the youngest disciple, it will not suffer us to continue immature or careless, but will impel us to the deepest spirituality and the most earnest and diligent conformity to all the will of God. There is nothing that has so chastening, humbling, heartsearching and sanctifying an influence over our spiritual life as to live a life of dependence upon Christ for our bodily strength from day to day.

Continuous Healing

There is another deeply spiritual truth connected with this discovery. Dr. Young translates the last clause of the passage in the continuous present tense; "I the Lord am healing thee." This is the aspect of divine healing which the apostle Paul so frequently emphasizes. It is not a mere fact or incident occurring occasionally in life, but it is a life of constant, habitual dependence upon Christ for the body. It is abiding in Him moment by moment for our physical, as well as spiritual, need. It is taking His resurrection life and strength for every breath and every step.

Attendant Blessings

Once more, the blessing that follows divine healing is finely expressed in the sequel to this ancient incident. "They came to Elim, where there were twelve springs and seventy palm trees, and they camped there near the water" (15:27). There is something exquisite about this sentence. It seems to be a sort of crystallized poem. The very tones fall upon the ear with strange sweetness. We can almost imagine that we feel the balm of the soft tropical air, hear the rustling of the palm trees and see the sparkling waters from Elim's wells. How refreshing the shade! How exhilarating the fountains! How delightful the rest! How heavenly the overshadowing cloud! It is like a scene from the land of Beulah.

It speaks to the deepest senses of the soul of the love life of the Lord and the peace of God that surpasses all understanding. And this is just the experience to which divine healing introduces the soul. The spiritual blessing is even richer than the physical. How real Christ seems to us. How we come to know the Lord as never before. How He rests us and sheds the fragrance of His love and joy through every sense of our spiritual and physical being until the heart finds utterance in the inspired song, "You prepare a table before me in the presence of my enemies. You anoint my head with oil; my cup overflows. Surely goodness and love will follow me all the days of my life, and I will dwell in the house of the LORD forever" (Psalm 23:5-6).

Friend, have you made this great discovery? It is hidden somewhere in your Bible. Perhaps the very trial that has crushed you is God's opportunity for revealing it to you. God grant that the old story may be reproduced in your life. "Moses cried out to the LORD, and the LORD showed him a piece of wood. He threw it into the water, and the water became sweet" (Exodus 15:25).

CHAPTER 2

Supernatural Life

Then Abraham prayed to God, and God healed Abimelech, his wife and his slave girls so they could have children again. (Genesis 20:17)

Against all hope, Abraham in hope believed and so became the father of many nations, just as it had been said to him, "So shall your offspring be." Without weakening in his faith, he faced the fact that his body was as good as dead—since he was about a hundred years old—and that Sarah's womb was also dead. Yet he did not waver through unbelief regarding the promise of God, but was strengthened in his faith and gave glory to God, being fully persuaded that God had power to do what he had promised. This is why "it was credited to him as righteousness." (Romans 4:18-22)

By faith Abraham, even though he was past age—and Sarah herself was barren—was enabled to become a father because he considered him faithful who had made the promise. (Hebrews 11:11)

We have here, from the old story of Genesis, three cases of divine healing: Abimelech, Abraham and Sarah. Abraham in a fit of unbelief consented to tell a half lie. Sarah was his half-sister, and he introduced her to Abimelech as his sister and left the way clear for him to take her as one of his many wives. God arrested Abimelech before he had done wrong.

The First Healing

God healed Abimelech through Abraham's prayer. No doubt they both made humble confession and together believed for God's deliverance, and God emphasized the answer by a distinct physical blessing. This is the earliest instance we have of faith and prayer for healing. It teaches us that sickness often comes as a divine chastening. And when the sin is laid aside, God takes away the chastening rod and heals the disease.

Abraham's Experiences

Alongside of this it is very natural for us to associate Abraham's and Sarah's faith for their physical quickening and the renewing of their youth and strength. It would seem as though Abraham's lesson with Abimelech strengthened his faith and threw him more directly upon God for his own personal need and blessing. We find in this transaction that both of them believed, and Sarah's faith is more emphatic even than Abraham's.

The construction of the Hebrews passage is very strong. It suggests that Sarah had made a bad failure at first and met the promise that she should be a mother with keen scorn and laughter at the very idea of such a thing. So it added that Sarah, "even Sarah" (KJV) as it is in the original, who had so failed, received supernatural strength to become the mother of Isaac. It shows that even if you did break down the first time you may still pick yourself up and overcome even if you have doubted. And surely there are none of us who have not had our doubts and fears. We know how patient and faithful God has been in restoring us and then teaching us through suffering the better way.

If you have been among the doubting ones, listen to God and let Him teach you. You may yet be among the royalty of faith as Abraham and Sarah were.

A Higher Kind of Strength

Divine healing is getting a new kind of life, and God values it more than He does natural strength. He did not want Isaac born through natural, but supernatural strength.

He gave divine strength to Abraham and Sarah, something that was a part of God Himself, because He wanted it to be of a higher order. Divine health is a better kind of health than the natural and it will accomplish a better kind of service for Christ. It is not the health that takes us to the ball game, the dance and theater, but the health that takes us to the slums, the alleys and garret. It is not only the divine message, but the messenger endued with divine strength and power.

So we have here the rudimentary principle, the very elementary and essential nature of divine healing. It is a higher sort of life. We believe for it, then we get it, and it leads to results more lasting and fruitful than the strength that we get from natural sources.

Abraham's Faith

In the fourth chapter of Romans, this very emphatic chapter of faith, Abraham alone is mentioned. In the first place he believed against hope. It was something that was not easy, not possible. Now this is essentially miraculous, and there is no doubt that God does sometimes override natural law in healing. I see no place in the Bible where we are taught that the miraculous is to cease with the ascension of the Lord. But we are told that the resurrection and ascension of Christ were the patterns according to which God was going to continue to work. We may know "his incomparably great power" (Ephesians 1:19) today. Do not be discouraged if God tells you to trust if everything is against it, even natural possibilities.

Again, we are told, and I like to read it both ways, each version gives a fine sense, that when he believed for this impossible thing "he considered not his own body" (KJV). He took his eyes and his attention off himself. If he had looked at it, perhaps it would have destroyed his faith. There are times when we must take our eyes off ourselves. We cannot stand while looking on the dark side. It is the devil that always says, "Pity yourself." He said it to Jesus Christ through Peter, and Jesus said to him, "Get behind me, Satan!" (Mark 8:33).

As Good as Dead

The Revised Version is still better and it gives a distinct thought: "Without being discouraged he considered his own body as good as dead" (Romans 4:19). That is, he put an estimate on it at the lowest value and then over against it he put the almightiness of God and said, "But God," doubting nothing. When God created the world He started with nothing. And there are times when He must smash us to pieces, for as long as there is the slightest ray of human hope we cling to it and do not get hold of God.

I have been very much afraid since my healing to count upon my strength. I do not consider myself strong—I do not care whether I am or not—but I found after the Lord had given me supernatural strength the enemy was getting me to trust in it. Then it left me and I had to very quickly get back to the old-fashioned way of depending upon Christ for my physical life and strength. It is counting yourself as good as dead, living each day as though it were a supernatural gift, taking His life by the moment. Do not be afraid to find yourself out in midair with nothing under you but the everlasting arms. Just look at the darkest and worst side of it and then look at God and say, "What does it matter?" It is just as easy for God to do a big thing as a little thing. He has His almightiness at His disposal and it is nothing for Him to use it, and indeed He wants to do so.

Do Not Stagger

Again, he "wavered not," "staggered not." Do not have a "perhaps," an "if," or a "but," about it. Do not allow anyone to sympathize with you. Many go through life wavering and staggering all the time. Abraham did not flinch, stagger or waver, but was "fully persuaded" that He who had promised was not only able, but, in the Greek, "abundantly able to perform," more than able, superfluously able to perform. His conception of God made it seem just like child's play for Him to do a great thing.

Again, there is a fine expression here—he not only did not stagger, but he "was strengthened in his faith" (4:20). The more he looked at the difficulties, and the more he looked at God, the stronger his faith waxed—growing all the time. The more he felt himself cut off from everything else the more he felt that God must help him. Are you waxing strong in faith?

Faith does not show what a man you are, but it shows what a God you have. The more we get from God the bigger beggars we are and the grander Father He is. That is, He puts us in a position where we must take a great deal and He is disappointed when we fail to do so.

Faith Glorifies God

I have read somewhere of a little street boy who was taken up out of a cellar by the Fresh Air Fund and sent to a farmer's house in Westchester (the county just north of New York City). He had a great big room all to himself. When he was shown into it at night and a little candle placed on the table, it was a perfect world of bewilderment to him and he thought he was in heaven. Finally he got tired and sleepy and looked at the snowy white bed. Why, he had never been in a bed in his life! So he slowly crept up to it, and after a while he just laid his little cheek against the soft pillow. He could not believe it was for him; there was some mistake. He began to feel guilty after a while. The idea that he should lie down on a white, snowy bed like that—it was presumption or intrusion. But he just went far enough to let his head poke into heaven for a moment. Then he got down on the floor under the bed and said: "This is the place for me," and curled himself up and was soon fast asleep. Early in the morning the landlady came in and saw him, and she cried, "Oh, dear me, what does the boy mean!" She picked him up, put him in the bed and tried to explain that the bed was for him. But she had the hardest time making him understand that he could get under the nice clean sheets.

How many of God's dear children there are who are sleeping under the bed instead of resting in the bosom of His love. We are so slow to believe all that He has for us and to take what we are entitled to. Oh, some day when whiter than the snow and higher than the angels, and when all the magnificence of the ages is at our feet, how ashamed we will be to think how hard it was for us to take a little crumb from our Father's table. God is looking for princely hearts, who, like Abraham, are willing to believe that He is the God that He says He is.

We cannot quite understand it, but it is so. Get it into your heart if you do not quite get it into your intellect and be strong in faith, giving glory to God. He has let that trouble come to you just for an opportunity to get you out of it, that it may be a stepping-stone to Himself.

CHAPTER 3

The Look That Brings Life

But the people grew impatient on the way.
(Numbers 21:4)

We so easily get discouraged and it is a most dangerous state to get in. It is the very place where the devil strikes us. Do not ever get discouraged.

The Wrong Way

The children of Israel had chosen their own way. God had told them it was a bad way before they had chosen it, but still they chose it. Therefore, they should not have gotten discouraged, because it was the way they wanted to go. Perhaps we are suffering from the results of disobedience, for having taken some way that God would not have chosen for us. But do not get discouraged, even if that is so, for God follows us and is there when we have brought our troubles upon ourselves. He will never leave us nor forsake us. Do not be discouraged by your trying situations. Do not look at these things; if you look at them they

15

will mesmerize you.

The children of Israel began to feel blue and to think things that were very bad. Do not ever let the devil know that he has hurt you. Do not ever let him hear you say, "It is hard." If he feels that he is hurting you he will stay and try harder, but if he thinks he isn't hurting you he will not waste his time on you. Do not for the world let people tell you about your troubles. Do not let them sympathize with you. Always rejoice, always be cheerful. Under no circumstances get discouraged or be depressed.

Unbelief

The next thing after they got discouraged, we read, "they spoke against God and against Moses, and said, 'Why have you brought us up out of Egypt to die in the desert? There is no bread! There is no water! And we detest this miserable food!'" (Numbers 21:5).

Discouragement leads to discontent: discontent leads to doubt, suspicion, unbelief. They did it under the disguise of giving Moses a good talking to, but it was God they were really addressing. The devil is trying today to get you to find fault with God. Don't hastily find fault with circumstances or with people, lest you should be found "fighting against God" (Acts 5:39).

Judgment

Next comes the stage of judgment. "Then the LORD sent venomous snakes among them; they bit

the people and many Israelites died" (Numbers
21:6). When we are looking for trouble we get
trouble. When we are in the complaining mood
we will get something to complain about. Oh, as
we talk about our little troubles if we could only
see what real trouble is. God often gives us a
pinch of it just to make us ashamed of our petty
complaining and murmuring.

So God sent judgment. God was very much
displeased with the spirit of murmuring, with the
spirit of discouragement, with the spirit of unbelief, and sent poisonous snakes. They were serpents, but God sent them. They were physical
ailments. They were demon powers. But God was
above; God was behind. Oh, how absurd and extreme are the teachings of the wildfire, self-ap-
pointed prophets of our age. God lets the devil be
an instrument of judgment. It is God's strange
way, but when people get on the devil's ground,
God lets the devil take them prisoners and shut
them up in the Castle of Giant Despair and makes
it very hard for them. God is in these troubles.
Disease may come from Satan or from natural
causes. It comes by divine permission. When you
find anybody talking lightly or recklessly about it,
just stick to your Bible. If God is in the chastening, God alone can command its removal.

Repentance

Next we find repentance. Judgment brings conviction, sorrow, shame, repentance. So they came
to Moses, and said, " 'We sinned when we spoke

against the LORD and against you. Pray that the LORD will take the snakes away from us.' So Moses prayed for the people" (21:7).

There must be frank acknowledgment of sin. Prayer must come after penitence—that is the place for Moses' prayer. And so we must pray. God hears the prayers of His united people and those whom He has placed in the ministry of a peculiar priesthood. The prayer does not dissipate the serpents. The prayer only sets in operation the process by which everything moves. God heard Moses' prayer, and He set in operation His plan of healing.

God's one object was to bring Jesus into prominence, to make Him known, to show Him in some new light and some new way. For this reason He let all this come to pass because He was going to give them a new emblem of His Son. So, dear friend, when sickness comes to you, when any trial enters into your life, even if it comes through your unbelief and sin, even if you have been to blame for it all, behind it all is the divine love that allows it to come into your life.

Revelation of Jesus

God lifts up His own Son in the midst of disease and death and bids them look to Him and live. If there has come to you a trial, even through a sin, lift up your eyes. You will behold not God's judgment, not a revelation of wrath, but a blessed manifestation of Jesus Christ. He will come into your life in some new way which you have never known before, and you will thank the devil and be glad of your trial for having brought you nearer to your Lord.

Moses was commanded to make a serpent of brass and set it upon a pole. And it came to pass that anyone who had been bitten could live by looking. God has told us that, "Just as Moses lifted up the snake in the desert, so the Son of Man must be lifted up" (John 3:14). This is God's remedy for disease as well as sin.

The Look of Faith

The prayer of Moses was not enough. The prayer of Moses brought the revelation of Jesus. But that was not enough unless they took the healing, looked at the figure and drew life from it by the contact of faith through the power of a look. It is just the same today. The prayers of God's people bring Christ to you, but you must take the life by the same look that they did. You must somehow get into contact with Him. The senses of your soul and the very functions of your body must somehow come into touch with Him, must become responsive to Him. Just draw from Him and drink from Him, just as the plant draws nourishment from the air and the soil and lives. It is a living touch and a living look.

Now this figure of looking is the most scientifically correct one that could be used. It is true that the eye has a strange power to bring into connection the outer with the inner world. If I look at an object of terror, it is infused into my mind, and there it is impressed as by a touch of fire. If that camera looks into your face, it takes your face right in. It just looks at you and it takes in all there is of you. So it is true, it is one of the strangest truths, that as we look at the evil the evil hypnotizes us, the evil imparts itself to us.

It is just the same when you turn heavenward. You reflect the brightness. You take in the joy and love and strength, and you grow like it and its nature passes into you.

So the wounded Hebrew looked at that bright image of brass and began to be conscious that a strange peace and sweetness was passing through his being, filling him with vital pulses from heart to limb, thrilling all his being. After a while the stupor and the horror of death passed away and he threw the serpent's poison off. But if he just curled himself up in his wretchedness and refused to look, all the pleadings of Moses were in vain.

That is just the way the woman was healed (Luke 8:43-48). She pressed forward and drew from the Lord the life that was in Him for anybody to take, but which the others did not know how to take. The same Christ is still lifted up, and the Holy Spirit loves to present Him in the hour of pain and sickness. If you turn to Him and fix your eye upon Him, then into the aching body will come peace and rest. You will find your lungs expanding, your frame exhilarated, and your lips will begin to say, "O Christ, Your flesh is food indeed, and Your blood is drink indeed." For it is not a glance, but it is a fixed and settled look. It is an abiding look. Now, this is where we come short; this is where we fall; this is the place to which nearly every case of disappointment can be traced. Perhaps you have confessed your wrong; perhaps you have believed in the divine remedy perhaps you have done it intelligently and believingly. But you did not keep Him in view. You did not begin to look and keep looking. You did not learn that inner touch, that blessed consciousness of the breath and the touch of Jesus Christ, that spiritual sense of God which He will give to the finest instincts of the trusting soul.

There is a strange disinclination to wait upon God. Men would rather go to a priest and give him money to do their waiting upon God for them instead of going to God themselves.

Christ's Atonement

Again, we are here taught the great atoning work of Jesus Christ for the body and for the soul. Why was it that this symbol of healing was made in the form of a serpent? Why wasn't some other symbol used? Why was the serpent chosen? It looks a little strange. There must have been some deep meaning in it. Was it not because our Savior was made in the likeness of sinful men? But the one point in which they differed was that the serpent of brass had no poison in it. He was made sin for us, but He was not sinful. He was made like the disease of the fallen race. There is something in Him that reminds us of our scourge and curse. But it did not really defile Him.

That serpent seems to point to the lifting up of the Son of Man on the cross. And it seems almost as if Jesus took the serpent right into His arms and received his poison and his sting that we might escape. Jesus took the serpent's sting and the serpent's poison into His own heart and into His own life, and, therefore, we may be free. Having borne in His body what our body deserves to bear, why should we bear it, too? Why should you be stung by the devil's fangs when He was stung to death for you? And so our Lord is revealed to us as the atonement for sickness, as the One who "took up our infirmities and carried our diseases" (Matthew 8:17), and "by his wounds we are healed" (Isaiah 53:5). The Holy Spirit is trying to present Him to you so that you cannot help seeing. Oh, for this revelation of Jesus! Oh, that He might come to you in the dark place, and the sad place, in the sick room, and say, "I have brought you here just so that your eyes might be turned to the cross."

If you just receive it, it will fill your being. But if you turn away it is gone. It is only while you look that you live. It is the abiding that keeps you in contact with the Living One. It will bind you up to Christ, and you will never be able to get along without Him. It will be true every moment that "apart from me you can do nothing" (John 15:5). Your life will be one long "[looking] on Jesus, the author and perfecter of our faith" (Hebrews 12:2).

CHAPTER 4

An Old Man Made Young

Now then, just as the LORD promised, he has kept me alive for forty-five years since the time he said this to Moses, while Israel moved about in the desert. So here I am today, eighty-five years old! I am still as strong today as the day Moses sent me out; I'm just as vigorous to go out to battle now as I was then. Now give me this hill country that the LORD promised me that day. You yourself heard then that the Anakites were there and their cities were large and fortified, but, the LORD helping me, I will drive them out just as he said. (Joshua 14:10-12)

We are to turn our attention first to the testimony of strength and health given by this venerable old servant of the Lord. And this is that he is as strong at 85 years as he was when he was only 40 years old. He could come and go as he pleased; he could put on his armor and fight. His Lord had kept him alive and sustained him all those years.

Strength for Life

First, it is strength for a lifetime that he tells us about—45 years of strength. It is a life sustained by the strength of God. That is so much better than a case of healing or some single deliverance from a hard trial. He wants to give us His very life, His health. Take Him for the habit of your life. Learn to live upon Him and have Him live in you. Then should emergencies come you will be able to get right up close to Him and be ready for anything. You will seldom have a hard trial if you take Him before the trial comes.

Privations

But again, we see here a life preserved in the midst of the greatest privations—the most inhospitable climate, the most depressing circumstances, burning sands, poisonous reptiles, inclement weather, the heat by day and the cold by night monotonous diet and the lack of water, the tremendous care and the special burden that rested on him. Caleb lived through all the wilderness experience. All the congregation but Joshua and Caleb passed away; they lived throughout. That was a splendid testimony of divine strength and life under the most unfavorable circumstances.

Again, it is the testimony of an old man made young; and of an old man who is as young as a boy, of strength that is unimpaired by years. Think of it, here was a man 85 years old just asking for a commission. When most are slowing down, Caleb was starting on the greatest campaign of his life. God says He will renew our strength like the eagle's, and He is wonderfully fulfilling this to some.

Again, we find here that it is not only spasmodic fits of strength, but the endurance of strength, that can stand a long pull and feel as fresh at the end as at the beginning. There are so many people who begin to step out, and soon begin to feel the shortness of breath and the painful reaction. But Caleb could stand it all day. God wants to give us that strength that can hold out all day, and still be good for many a day and year. God will give you the strength that will stand, and be as fresh tomorrow as it was today.

But once again, look at Caleb's courage. Sometimes when strength does not fail, the spirit fails, and we lie off and do not venture as much as in other days. You know the picture in Ecclesiastes of the old man who is "afraid of heights" (12:5). He does not like to go upstairs; he does not like to work too much; he is afraid of hurting himself. Things look bigger than they are and he makes up his mind that he is weak. Do not lose courage. Do not be laid aside. God will keep you sweetly working for Him until your life work is done. I think it is beautiful to look at this venerable old man, as fresh as a boy, brave and full of holy confidence and just asking for the hardest job, that He could prove how much God could do.

The Secret

Let us look in the next place and see from whence it came, the secret of it. He tells us that it was not his constitution or the care he took of himself. But he says, "The Lord, my God, has kept me alive." It all came directly from a divine source. He had learned the meaning of that old covenant, "I am Jehovah Ropha; I will be your continuous support and the source of your life moment by moment." So Caleb had gone to Him and He had not failed. Even when God does heal us there is so much danger of our getting to depend on the feeling of strength and the health we have, instead of constantly taking it freshly from the same source in God. We have so often seen people when they are raised up from sickness, detach their faith from God to themselves, and because they feel so well, they conclude they are well. You have been looking at the pitcher rather than the spring. Get right back to the spring and stay there.

Followed Fully

Once again, we have here the conditions as well as the source of Caleb's wonderful strength and health: "because [Caleb has] followed the LORD my God wholeheartedly" (Joshua 14:9). It came from God, but it came from God for a reason. He met the conditions and God fully met him. Not because he had followed, but because he had "followed . . . wholeheartedly."

The difference between the genius and the man of commonplace ability lies in things that are not at first perceived. The value of that painting just lies in the little art touches. So the power of the Holy Spirit in your life and mine, and the measure of our obedience and intimacy with God must come up to following God wholly, or we will miss much. A single splash of ink on that fine dress, and the dress is destroyed. One little link broken in the chain, and the chain is no good. So a seeming trifle may spoil all your blessing.

In the letter to the Hebrews, it is not faith that the apostle requires; it is a particular kind of faith. He says, "do not throw away your confidence" (10:35), that is, the faith of boldness, of audacity. Remember the faith of Abraham that Paul speaks about. It was a kind of faith that had no "wavering" in it. "He did not waver through unbelief regarding the promise of God" (Romans 4:20).

Remember the faith that was spoken of in the gospel of Matthew. Jesus said, "If you have faith as small as a mustard seed . . . nothing will be impossible for you" (17:20-21). There are lots of people who have faith, but they just hold back a little. They believe up to a certain point, but there is a "but" and an "if " and a "perhaps" and a reserve. So their surrender reaches a certain point and stops there, and their joy and their peace depend to a certain extent upon circumstances. Not so with Caleb, he "followed the LORD [his] God wholeheartedly" (Joshua 14:9). Therefore, the Lord was wholly with him.

Fully Believed

How did he wholly follow the Lord? First, he wholly believed God. He believed God without any kind of reservation. God told him to go and spy out the land, and he came back and told them just what the Lord had told him. "It is a beautiful land. God is with us. Let us go up at once, and possess it. For we are well able to overcome it."

Does God require us to have that kind of faith? Yes, friend, He does. He requires that when you pray you will believe you have the thing you ask for. How in the world will we ever do it? Why, we never could do it, but Jesus does it for us. He teaches us to throw away the faith we have and take His instead. If He gives it, it will be as perfect as His own.

I am so glad that I am not bringing to you an impossible task. Oh, let us find out what the crucified life means. It is the life that comes to the conclusion forevermore that you are no good, and never will be. "The life I live, . . . I live by faith in the Son of God" (Galatians 2:20). Just find it out, friend, and it will be unspeakably delightful to know that Jesus is your all and in all. You will find that He is "the author and perfecter of our faith" (Hebrews 12:2). But, He does require of you that your faith have no "ifs" nor "buts" about it. Will you have it?

And so again, Caleb not only believed fully, but he followed the Lord wholly in witnessing for Him. He not only believed, but he said he believed. He stood up in the camp alone and still said it. And when the camp turned upon him in an angry crowd and said they would stone him, he still said it, and God blessed him for it.

Waited

Not only did he witness, but he waited, for faith must learn to wait. Forty-five years was a long time, but his faith did not fail to wait. It stood the long pull as well as the strong pull. God said, "I will give you every place where you set your foot" (Joshua 1:3). And for 45 years he kept his eye on Hebron, and said, "I cannot afford to die, for I have something to live for; I have a promise, and that is something to live for." It is a great thing to have a goal before you. Caleb had one, and he waited and waited, and finally won it. Not only did he follow God but he put himself in a place where he must have special strength from God. He put himself in a place where God must carry him through or bring dishonor upon Himself.

Do not venture unless you have the faith, but if you have you will do something. You will go out to meet the mighty Lord and He will meet you. I am sure God is searching our hearts today and putting us upon our faces, and making us glad we have Jesus Christ to be our all and in all. Do not merely talk about it. Get somewhere! Do something for God! Make your healing a blessing and a power in the world. Make it worth God's while to bless you.

CHAPTER 5

The Cleansing of the Leper

(Leviticus 14)

The leper was God's object lesson of the effect of sin upon the body. It was the picture of evil within stamping its likeness upon the whole frame. And so in the healing of this leper we have the very principles of the gospel of Jesus Christ, as it deals with the double question of sin and sickness. You must always associate the two together. The leper stood before the priest crying: "Unclean, unclean," and the poor fellow bore the stamp of his uncleanness. It is all presented in great fullness in the 14th chapter of the book of Leviticus.

Christ Comes to Us

First, the priest goes to him outside the camp. Here we find Jesus Christ, of whom this priest was the type, not waiting for us to get fixed up and come up to the level where He can heal us, but coming down to the level where we are and lifting us up to Him.

Yes, He will come to you. He will be your righteousness and lead you every step of the way. And although you may be a sinful, paralyzed, unclean leper, He is your High Priest and will come to you just where you are and help and heal you.

The first step always is Jesus. "I am the way" (John 14:6). "Tell me the way to Jesus," somebody said. And there never was a better answer: "There is no way to Jesus, for Jesus is the Way. There is nothing for you to do before you get to Jesus. Jesus is the first thing, Jesus the next thing."

The Cross

Then the next thing we see in the story of this leper brings us up to the cross and the Crucified One. It is the sweet picture of the death and resurrection of Christ presented by two little birds that were to be brought, the one sacrificed and the other set at liberty. The first little bird was to be killed, and we know what that means, the death of the Lord Jesus Christ through which our cleansing and our healing come. The cleansing of the leper was through the blood of the little bird. Your cleansing and healing are through the blood of the Lord Jesus Christ—the death of Christ. It is the greatest fact in the history of the world, and it is fitting that we should fully take it in. You can cry over the passion of Christ. That will not make you a better man or a better woman. It is faith that must enter in and take the real meaning. It means, my dear friend, when He died that afternoon, you died and I died. That was the end of the old I, the sinful, guilty self.

God does not take the old man and fix him and cleanse him. The old man is put away. That is the meaning of resurrection life. It does not mean that our natural strength is improved a little, but our natural strength is as good as dead. It is crucified with Christ. It means that we have taken another kind of life—the life of the risen Son of God. It is not our strength increased, but it is our strength displaced and God's strength given instead.

The Resurrection

Not only is it the death of the little bird; do not dwell too long on that. Quickly you are carried right along in the double action of the figure to the other little bird that was held beneath the dripping blood of the dead bird, sprinkled with its blood, and covered with the drops of its life. Then all crimson and stained and baptized into the death of the dead one, it was set free in the open field and went singing away in its glad liberty, a picture of the resurrection. One bird could show the dead Christ, but it took the other bird to show the living Christ. So this other little bird tells us that we are cleansed and healed by the resurrection of our Lord. It tells us that we may enter into the partnership of His death just as the living bird did. It was just baptized into the death of Jesus Christ, buried with Him in baptism. Then we are to go free, just as if we were another being born out of Him, and alive forevermore. For a moment you see the flowing blood and the gasping bird, but in another moment you hear the glad cry of the living bird and the triumphant song of freedom and life.

It is a cross where He hangs no more. It is a grave where He lies no more. It is a vacant cross. It is an empty tomb. It is a living Christ.

I do not know of any finer picture of the true meaning of the cross and resurrection than that of the sculptor who cut in marble a cross. But he immediately covered it up by twisting around it a beautiful vine. He hung the leaves and the clusters so thick upon it that you could scarcely tell the cross was there. There had been a cross, but over it hung the thick, rich clusters of leaves and fruit of the vine. And so the death of Christ is now covered over with the fruit of His risen life, and Easter ought to be to us a glad, bright, glorious new year of the heart and of the life; the resurrection rather than the death, the death only as a pathway to the resurrection. It is the life of Christ that makes us pure, happy and well.

Listen to Him as He cries: "A spirit doesn't have flesh and bones, as you see me have. Handle me and see." Bones, flesh, a man, human every whit! And "we are members of his body, of his flesh, and of his bones" (Ephesians 5:30, KJV). It is the risen Christ. He is your head. He is your very heart. He is your true life. He shares with you His life. And so right here in the cleansing of the leper we have this other picture, the death and resurrection of the Lord as the secret of our life both for soul and body.

The story of this leper is carried on through a series of deeper processes which we can only touch upon.

Deeper Life

First, we have the washing of his clothes. That means the habits of our lives. Then there is the washing of himself. That is not only the outward but the inward life. And then there is another process, the shaving of the hair on his head, and even his beard and his eyebrows. It was a very keen and a very heart-searching process. The hair means our own strength. It is the type of human strength, and here we are taught what it really means to die with Christ. It is not to die to your evil habits only and your evil nature, but it is to die especially to your strength, to your confidence, to your self-sufficiency and especially to your own opinions and ideas. The hair on your head, your intellectual mind, your eyebrows, the way you look at things. Oh, how we have to die to all this before Christ can heal us! What a revolution we have to pass through, until we see as He sees and lose confidence in our views and judgments.

Consecration

And then a little later comes that other beautiful rite—the dipping of the finger of the priest in the blood of the sacrifice and applying it three times to the leper; first, to the right ear, next to his thumb and then to his foot. It is just a touch of the blood to the ear, the organ of hearing; the hand, the organ of activity and action. The feet, the members with which we walk.

The blood always means the life. The life is in the blood, and it means the life of Jesus. Divine life—the personal life of the Son of God—has come to our brains, our minds, our hands, our activities, our feet, our walk, our life.

The Anointing

And then after the blood had come, the oil followed. This meant something more than the life, for the oil represents the Holy Spirit. You need the Holy Spirit to possess you, to give you power. It is possible to have the life without the power. The oil means power. "You will receive power when the Holy Spirit comes on you" (Acts 1:8)—effectual life, life with power behind it.

The Filling

And then there is just one more type. He uses the remnant of the oil—all that is left is to be poured upon the head of him who is to be cleansed. That is the filling with the Holy Spirit, coming into every part of your being, getting in the utmost possible measure God's highest thought and will.

Here we have in this little picture the whole story of redemption for the soul, spirit and body. Could there be anything harder than the case of that leper? Your case is not worse. But could there be anything higher than the height to which he is raised, for this beautiful picture carries him on and up until he is filled with all the fullness of the Holy Spirit. And all this is brought right down to our level! All this is waiting for us through our great High Priest, who is coming forth to us outside the camp and is now waiting to bless us!

CHAPTER 6

The Message of Elihu

(Job 33)

The story of Job belongs to the patriarchal age. It is an object lesson of the great principles of God's government. Job stands before us as an example of a good man, a man who has reached the highest ideals of his own time. He is a godly man, but a man who has not yet been thoroughly crucified to his own strength and goodness, and has not entered into that deeper experience which we know is the resurrection life. We find Abraham passing through it in his sacrifice of Isaac on Mount Moriah. We find Joseph passing through it in his years of anguish. We find Moses and David passing through it, and here we have the story of Job. This sudden trial, for which there seems to be no explanation, comes to him. While it lasts and before he comes out in his marvelous victory, God lets it come before us in a drama in which all the light and help that man can give to his fellow man passes away in failure.

Failure

First, we have Job's own wife who fails, utterly fails, and at last in despair bids him give the whole thing up.

Then we see the three worldly friends pass by one after the other, each representing some phase of human wisdom. One represents the wealth of the world, another represents the wisdom of the world, and the other represents the goodness of the world. Each one thinks he knows all about it. Before they got through they had to come and ask God's forgiveness, and then Job's, for their rashness, their blindness, their stupidity.

But they have to appear and then fail. And finally Job has to fail. He thought he was all right, maintained his integrity and stuck to it that he was not to blame. But even Job had to break down at last. His righteousness had to fail. God had to lay him in the dust until he abhorred himself and repented in dust and ashes. Then God Himself appeared as the explanation and the remedy for all, and Job was lifted up and restored to all that he had before. And the whole drama was made plain that what God wanted was to show the vanity of all human helpers and even Job's goodness, and then give him something better—His own righteousness.

The Voice of God

But now right here before the close of the drama, before the climax, this man Elihu appears upon the scene. After all others have talked themselves empty and Job has answered them, Elihu, a young man, steps forward and claims to be the voice and inspiration of the Almighty. His wise and wonderful message seems to bear it all out. While the whole book is inspired in a sense, yet all the speakers previously have just talked vanity and wind. Elihu is the first who speaks the thought of the deep spiritual teachings of the New Testament. It is very much like the 12th chapter of Hebrews. It unfolds the highest and holiest principles of God's government in dealing with His children and is far in advance of anything we find even in the Mosaic teachings.

First he tells us that God is always trying to talk to men. His object is to reach their consciences and their hearts. "For God does speak—now one way, now another—though man may not perceive it" (Job 33:14). He does everything that He can to make men understand. Through the Holy Spirit He tries to bring to them conviction and to hold them back from His purpose, and "keep [man] from pride" (33:17). That is, that He may arrest you in some wrong attitude or action and humble in you some form of pride which is to bring you to ruin.

God is trying to make us understand, and He is taking the gentler methods first. He does not want to resort to severity, but to guide us with His eye. So He puts thoughts into our minds, He puts fears upon our hearts and brings various influences to bear. He is the God of providence and interposes in all the events of life. He speaks to us by His gracious deliverances and He tries to have us escape some severer lesson. We read in the 18th verse, He "[preserves] his soul from the pit, his life from perishing by the sword." He kindly delivers us from the danger and lets us see His providential working. Many times God has interposed just that we might understand that He loves us.

God's Second Voice

Still man does not learn, still God's love and kindness seem to be wasted, and now the severe testings have to come. "A man may be chastened on a bed of pain with constant distress in his bones, . . . His flesh wastes away to nothing, and his bones, once hidden, now stick out" (33:19, 21).

Sickness comes, terrible sickness, sickness that seems to make every bone ache with keen pain, so that his appetite fails, his flesh is consumed and his bones all seem to stick out. They say he must die; there is no hope for him. His friends give him up. The physicians give him up. There is nothing seemingly but the grave. This is the hardest sort of a case. And yet he tells us that God's hand has been in all this. No talk of the devil here at all. The hand of providence is in it all, God's hand. Do not run into wild fire. Stick to your Bible. God uses sickness. God uses trial. He lets the devil have a part in it. But it is by God's permission that all this has come. Perhaps it is a long story. Perhaps it has taken months, perhaps years, to bring him to this condition.

The Messenger

Well now, what next? Ah, here is the halting place where God brings His next agency. Providence stops for a moment, and now grace comes in. "Yet if there is an angel on his side"—in other words, if there is somebody who understands God's way, that His end is always mercy and His purpose always blessing, "to tell a man what is right for him" (33:23)—this speaks of someone to show him God's uprightness, to show him what God's purpose is, to help him to understand God, to submit to God, to listen to God, to put himself in God's hands. If there is only somebody there with a gentle, loving hand, and a faithful touch to press through all the films and help him to get to the heart of God, then, oh, what a change!

The Atonement

Then he is "gracious to him and [says], 'Spare him from going down to the pit; I have found a ransom for him' " (33:24). So here in the very heart of the patriarchal age we have this word. He has been all wrong, but God has a way of making it right, through the very blood of Christ's redemption. Jesus has redeemed us from the curse of the law, being made a curse for us. We see this all through the Mosaic teaching. We saw it earlier when we were talking about the leper and the two little birds that were used for his cleansing. We saw it in the brazen serpent that was raised on the pole. We have it in the censer of Aaron swinging between the living and the dead. So here we have it, right in the beginning of the Old Testament, the Ransom, Jesus Christ, making settlement on account of our body, substituting His stripes for our sickness and healing us by them.

The Healing

So this intercessor sits down by Job and tells him about God and then comes the healing. There is no waste of words, but just one sentence: "His flesh is renewed like a child's; it is restored as in the days of his youth" (33:25). It is not merely healing. It is regeneration. It is "a converted body." It is life given back in all its freshness. It is not an old man made well, but it is a new heart put into his being and new blood into his veins. It is a renewing of life. It is the deeper teaching of the resurrection life. Not the repair shop tinkering you up and letting you go on a little longer in the old break-down way, but it is that something which He is bringing to us in these days, the childhood of nature. It is that deep, sweet love life of the Lord which He wants to pour into all our being and make us young again.

There is something about this picture of healing that is delightful: "renewed like a child," a buoyant freshness that makes you return to the days of your youth. God wants to make you like a happy, trusting child, and make it so delightful both to Him and you that you will feel it is joy to have

Him heal you. He now brings you to a place of closer communion: "He prays to God and finds favor with him, he sees God's face and shouts for joy" (33:26). You will be brought into a new, sweet place. He will deliver your "soul from going down to the pit, and [you] will live to enjoy the light" (33:28).

Elihu tells us that God often deals thus with men. His real purpose is to make them understand Him, to get them right with Him, and then bless them outwardly as well as inwardly. It is the 12th chapter of Hebrews, the third epistle of John. It is the soul and body prospering and being in health conjointly. We should look into our own lives, our own needs, and understand our Father's love. How stupid we have been, how slow and how often we have tried to run from Him!

God Always Teaching

When God is dealing with His children He usually has some deeper lesson for each time. Perhaps you have learned the former lesson and He is now teaching you something more, and the process may be a little slow and a little long. God has something to say that you have not yet heard.

The whole key to this passage seems to be, God speaking and man not understanding. "Man may not perceive it" (33:14). Perhaps you have learned the lesson of your first and second healing, and now He has something else to teach you. There is a strange, sweet reluctance upon His part here. He speaks once, or even twice, before He brings sickness. And then He is so quick to remove it if we will open our ears and turn our hearts to Him. Never let us lose confidence in His perfect love. He does not want to break our spirit, or let it get hard, resentful or discouraged. He loves us, forevermore, and He wants us to trust His love and through His love to get hold of His life.

CHAPTER 7

Samson, an Object Lesson
in Divine Healing

*But he said to me, "You will conceive and give
birth to a son. Now then, drink no wine or other
fermented drink and do not eat anything unclean, because the boy will be a Nazirite of God
from birth until the day of his death."*

*The woman gave birth to a boy and named
him Samson. He grew and the LORD blessed him,
and the Spirit of the LORD began to stir him
while he was in Mahaneh Dan, between Zorah
and Eshtaol. (Judges 13:7, 24-25)*

Samson was marked from birth by the Spirit
of the Lord coming upon him. This was
characteristic throughout a period of his life. We
read in Judges 14:6: "The Spirit of the LORD
came upon him in power so that he tore the lion
apart with his bare hands as he might have torn
a young goat." And again in the 19th verse,
"Then the Spirit of the LORD came upon him in
power. He went down to Ashkelon, struck down

thirty of their men, [and] stripped them of their belongings."

Separation

In the dark days of the Judges, God brings out this striking object lesson of divine life for the body. Just as He had linked the principle of sickness with sin in the case of the leper, so here He links purity and strength, physical power with right living and separation to God. The first principle brought out here is that the foundation of strength is separation unto God. He was a Nazirite from his mother's womb. And so, in order to be separated from every unclean thing, his mother must not even eat anything unclean. Both she and Samson must also abstain from wine and strong drink.

This seems to have special reference to earthly passion and desire. The spirit of true restraint and moderation is closely connected with a sound and healthy condition. Therefore, it was not only a life of purity, but a life of true victory over self—the crucified life, the life that died to earthly things. God wants you to be pure, and God wants you to be subdued, to be self-restrained. Not that there is any gospel of asceticism, but the true principle of life is, " 'Everything is permissible for me'—but I will not be mastered by anything" (1 Corinthians 6:12). I will not allow myself unduly to care for anything, for as soon as it gets the mastery over me then it becomes wrong. The thing that might be right for you at one time is not best at another

time. And so before the strong physical life of
Samson could be developed he had to be a Nazirite in the true sense of the word. Then the simplicity of his life appears in the fact that no razor
was to touch him. He was not to think of personal
adornment.

Strength

Next we find in Samson, not only the principle
of purity, but the principle of supernatural
strength, the physical life that simply comes from
a source outside of his physical organism. Men
look for evolution by natural laws. They do not
expect any more to come out of a thing than they
see go in. Here is a kind of strength that is unac-
countable, that has no philosophy behind it. There
is no reason why it should exist. Where does it
come from?

We are told again and again in these Old Testament records, that there may be no mistake, "the
Spirit of the LORD," the breath of God, came upon
this man. This shouldn't be entirely new to us, for
that was the way it was in the beginning: "God . . .
breathed into [man's] nostrils the breath of life"
(Genesis 2:7).

The Spirit of God began to move Samson.
There came manifestations, paroxysms of supernatural energy, and he would do things that were
even a wonder to himself. After a while the consciousness settled down upon him, and he knew
that he had in him a strange secret of physical energy that others did not possess. When the lion

came upon him, he just tore it in two as if it were a kid. He took the gates of Gaza and carried them off on his shoulders. And before his life was over, he tore down the colossal temple of the Philistines upon the heads of his enemies. There was nothing in bone or muscle that could explain it. It was just a paroxysm of force that swept into him from a divine source.

Spiritual Force

What God once did He can do again. He does not do these things for play. He does not bring out a character like Samson so that we may gaze at him like a star. God's highest method of working still is to put into human bodies a kind of physical energy for which there is no way of accounting apart from the Holy Spirit. It is God's normal idea for us that the Spirit of God should move upon us and stir us with physical forces that take away the disease and give us powers of endurance that even we cannot understand. This is why Samson lived this strange supernatural life. God raised him up to show you that if a man will clear the way for God by keeping out of unwholesome influences, by getting on the ground of purity, God will just pour through him celestial dynamite. It is not so much better machinery that you want as more power to run it.

The other day we found our office in a state of collapse, and everything suspended because an engine had gone to pieces and the power that turned the printing presses was still. The machinery would not go; the engine had refused to work. Power, power, power was all we wanted. Then everything went all right.

And so in your life and mine. Do not try to fix up your heart and your joints and your indigestion, but get power, get the engine going. Let the heavenly current charge you and everything will go. You want a supernatural addition to the force you have. You have natural power when things are all regular, but when they begin to get irregular you must have twice as much power. Get God into the machinery, and even if it is a little rusty and a little stiff, it will become sufficient if the power is there.

That is the idea of Samson. I do not want to exaggerate the picture, but there it looms, a great gigantic figure in the darkest ages of history. God's example of a body charged by a divine battery—with the life of the Holy Spirit.

Friend, have you received a physical baptism of the Holy Spirit? Your mind has been baptized with the Spirit. Your affections have been baptized with the Spirit. Do you know what it is for your physical consciousness just to breathe in the rest and quietness of this divine inspiration? Have you received the Holy Spirit into your body? You have been in the third chapter of First Corinthians. Have you ever definitely entered into the sixth chapter of First Corinthians? Take it to your hearts. Ask God to make it real to you, and, oh, when it comes to pass, you can understand the mystery of Samson's life. It will not be a mystery anymore. You will say a hundred times a day, "Is it not wonderful, is it not blessed to have something inside of you that you cannot explain. But it moves you, it makes you run for God and almost fly for God.

That is the second principle then in the history of Samson. First, it means a separated life from every evil thing that could hurt you, and then it means a strong life deriving energy from a source outside and above.

Unseen Forces

We might show this through the natural world. That force and power, even in the universe, is not in matter, but it is in a principle behind matter. You cannot see it; you cannot feel it. Take the subject of gravity. I need not tell you that the law of gravity is the greatest force we know. But you cannot see it. You cannot take it in your hand. You can take electricity and bottle it up. You cannot do this with gravity, but it is the greatest force there is. Those particles of granite cling together by an unseen force, a kind of spiritual or ethereal force. The most advanced science is unable to tell anything about it. Nobody knows what gravity is. It is a power you cannot see, but it is the greatest power of nature. And so we might follow all through the natural world, and find it is not the visible things, but the invisible things that are strong.

God has just given us parables all through nature to show us that He wants to raise us above the material. He wants us to see the thing behind the thing we see. He wants us to get to God Himself. Perhaps when they find out the secret of nature, they will find that it is the living God, for "in him all things hold together" (Colossians 1:17). He is wanting us to learn that in our bodies. He wants us to glorify these earthly temples by filling them with something grander and better.

Not It, but Him

So many people are wanting the "thing" to go; wanting "it," whatever that "it" is, inside or outside. There are all sorts of "its." You want something that will make you feel better. I do not believe that is what God wants. God wants you to get your eye off of these things and place it on Him. And soon you will have so much of Him you will not have time to watch "it." And if God wants you to live a year with something hurting you, and all that time be so strong that nobody will understand it, all right, let it stay. Just get your thoughts centered on the Holy Spirit, on God Himself. Let things go. Let the devil fight. Let all be upside down. Never mind, if you and God are right.

What does this lesson mean? It means, first, clear the way for God. If you had a wire overhead that was partly wire and partly hemp, you would not get any electricity. It must be all wire. So if you let your body be partly God's and partly the flesh's, partly the world's, why, it will be hindered. The first thing is right of way for God.

Use His Power

The second thing is, perhaps, to be fully persuaded, intelligently persuaded of the glorious ministry of the Holy Spirit for the body as well as the soul. Then the next thing is to do as the scientist does, as the intelligence of our modern age does with the hidden forces of nature. They used to let the lightning kill men, but now they take it and harness it and use it. Today men have found out that lightning is the most beneficent power of the universe and they use it. Now, get to work and study the laws of the Holy Spirit. Find out all the modes of His operation, the things that help to bring Him. Then adjust yourself to Him and you will find out that the Spirit of God will fit into your life as perfectly as the power fits into our machinery.

Finally, do not get it all in theory. Go ahead and practice it, and the Holy Spirit will teach you how to use it. And after a while you will have it all in experience, and you will find what an all-round Friend He is. There is not a thing in your life-work to which He cannot adjust Himself—social life, brain work, everything. He will just be the God of your life. Study Him. Find out the laws of His working. Adjust yourself to Him. And then use His glorious resources.

CHAPTER 8

Divine Healing in the Psalms

The Hebrew Psalter is the manual of religious experience for the children of God in every age. We may therefore expect that its rich devotional pages will express the physical conflicts and blessings of the trusting heart as well as the deeper and more spiritual states. We are not disappointed.

A Sedative

What is more necessary to physical health and comfort than sleep? And so we find the psalmist like a tired and trusting child leaning upon his Father and often echoing the sentiment of Psalm 127:2, "he grants sleep to those he loves." This is better than all the sedatives and narcotics of medical science. We have not learned far in the blessed gospel of healing if we have not yet learned the secret of going to sleep in the arms of our Lord. How finely this is expressed in these two passages in the early psalms of David, "I will lie down and sleep in peace, for you alone, O LORD, make me dwell in safety" (4:8). And the other is but the echo of it, "I lie down and sleep; I wake again, because the LORD sustains me" (3:5).

Psalm 6

Our next reference is a prayer for healing: "Be merciful to me, LORD, for I am faint; O LORD, heal me, for my bones are in agony. . . . I am worn out from groaning; all night long I flood my bed with weeping and drench my couch with tears" (6:2, 6). This is indeed a bitter cry, but it is soon changed into a joyful song of praise. "Away from me, all you who do evil, for the LORD has heard my weeping. The LORD has heard my cry for mercy; the LORD accepts my prayer" (6:8-9).

Psalm 18

We turn over a few pages and we come to the Psalm 18, which is a sublime record of answered prayer. "It is God," he cries, "who arms me with strength and makes my way perfect. . . . He trains my hands for battle; my arms can bend a bow of bronze" (18:32, 34). David's physical prowess and victorious strength in battle were not due to the practiced muscles of the athlete, but to the supernatural power that fired his veins with divine strength and made his battles the battles of the Lord. The same strength is still available for those who trust in Him. In the consciousness of His power our lives may be multiplied tenfold.

Psalm 27

Here is a fine burst of praise for physical life

and deliverance from danger and from death: "I am still confident of this: I will see the goodness of the LORD in the land of the living" (27:13). It was not in the land of the hereafter but in the land of the living that he believed to see the goodness of the Lord. And he saw it.

Psalm 30

In Psalm 30 we have again the double side of prayer and praise.

> O LORD my God, I called to you for help
>   and you healed me.
> O LORD, you brought me up from the
>   grave;
>   you spared me from going down into the
>   pit.
>
> Weeping may remain for a night,
>   but rejoicing comes in the morning.
>
> You turned my wailing into dancing;
>   you removed my sackcloth and clothed
>   me with joy. (30:2-3, 5, 11)

Psalm 32

Psalm 32 is also a testimony of pardon and healing.

> When I kept silent,
>   my bones wasted away
>   through my groaning all day long.

For day and night
 your hand was heavy upon me;
my strength was sapped
 as in the heat of summer.
Then I acknowledged my sin to you
 and did not cover up my iniquity.
I said, "I will confess
 my transgressions to the LORD"—
and you forgave
 the guilt of my sin.

You are my hiding place;
 you will protect me from trouble
 and surround me with songs of
  deliverance. (32:3-5, 7)

Psalm 34

Psalm 34 is one of the favorite "Ebenezers" of every victorious life. It tells of deliverance both from troubles and from fears. There is one precious promise in it that some of us have literally proved in hours of peril. "He protects all his bones, not one of them will be broken. . . . The LORD redeems his servants; no one will be condemned who takes refuge in him" (34:20, 22).

Psalm 39

Here is a humbler and more sorrowful prayer that sometimes fits into the hour of deep depression.

Remove your scourge from me;
 I am overcome by the blow of your hand.

You rebuke and discipline men for their sin;
    you consume their wealth like a moth—
    each man is but a breath.

Look away from me, that I may rejoice
        again
before I depart and am no more.
        (39:10-11, 13)

But the next psalm very soon turns the prayer into praise. "I waited patiently for the LORD; he turned to me and heard my cry. . . . He put a new song in my mouth, a hymn of praise to our God" (40:1, 3).

Psalm 41

Next we come to one of the sweetest of the psalms—one that ought to be hung up in every chamber of sickness and pain. "The LORD will sustain him on his sickbed and restore him from his bed of illness" (41:3). How gentle His care! How paternal His nursing! How thoughtful His provision for the turning of our very couch, when, as sometimes happens, the trial lingers.

Psalm 42

Psalm 42 has a fine expression in the 11th verse, "Put your hope in God, for I will yet praise him, my Savior [the health of my countenance, KJV] and my God." It is repeated in the following psalm and it may well suggest the bright and shining face which God's health gives to the countenance, and which we should ever wear as our testimony to Him.

Psalm 50

"Call upon me in the day of trouble; I will deliver you, and you will honor me" (50:15). This is a promise which may well cover every day of trouble and every case of sickness, need and pain.

Psalm 51

"Let me hear joy and gladness; let the bones you have crushed rejoice" (51:8). Here we see that spiritual trouble brings on us physical prostration and distress and that forgiveness and blessing bring healing and comfort to the mortal frame.

Psalm 55

Where can we find a darker picture of the sinking life than in Psalm 55?

> My heart is in anguish within me;
>   the terrors of death assail me.
> Fear and trembling have beset me;
>   horror has overwhelmed me.
> I said, "Oh, that I had the wings of a dove!
>   I would fly away and be at rest." (55:4-6)

But soon we hear once more the sweeter notes of praise,

> But I call to God,
>   and the LORD saves me.
> He ransoms me unharmed
>   from the battle waged against me,
>   even though many oppose me.

Cast your cares on the Lord
  and he will sustain you;
  he will never let the righteous fall.
    (55:16, 18, 22)

Psalm 56

Again in Psalm 56, we have another testimony of God's deliverance from death. "I will present my thank offerings to you. For you have delivered me from death and my feet from stumbling, that I may walk before God in the light of life" (56:12-13).

Psalm 63

There is a fine expression in the first verse of Psalm 63: "My body longs for you." There is such a thing as the crying out of our physical being to God for quickening and strength. Just as a baby lives on the life of its mother, so God is the supply of all our life. "Man does not live on bread alone, but on every word that comes from the mouth of God" (Matthew 4:4). David had learned this deep secret of the divine life, and it is because of this that Christ has become for us the Living Bread, that he who eats Him will live by Him.

Psalms 68, 71 and 73

Praise be to the Lord, to God our Savior,
  who daily bears our burdens.

Our God is a God who saves;

from the Sovereign LORD comes escape
from death. (68:19-20)

I will come and proclaim your mighty acts,
O Sovereign LORD;
I will proclaim your righteousness, yours
alone.

Though you have made me see troubles,
many and bitter,
you will restore my life again;
from the depths of the earth
you will again bring me up.
You will increase my honor
and comfort me once again. (71:16, 20-21)

My flesh and my heart may fail,
but God is the strength of my heart
and my portion forever.

Yet I am always with you;
you hold me by my right hand. (73:26, 23)

All these are testimonies of the healing and
strengthening touch of God.

General Promises

There are general promises in the Scriptures
and in the psalms which cover all our needs, including the healing of our bodies. Such a promise
is Psalm 84:11, "For the LORD God is a sun and
shield; the LORD bestows favor and honor; no

good thing does he withhold from those whose walk is blameless."

Psalm 91

But it is needless to say the richest and fullest of the psalms of help and healing is the 91st. It almost reads like a psalm of Moses. The drapery of it reminds one of the tabernacle and the Holy of Holies, the secret place of the Almighty. Let's look at three things in this beautiful psalm.

I. What God Himself is

1. He is the Most High, above all other power and therefore above all adversaries and evils.
2. He is the Almighty. This is the mighty Shaddai, the God who is sufficient.
3. He is a refuge and fortress, that is, the One to whom we fly in times of danger, either for offensive or defensive warfare.
4. He is our habitation, for having found Him a shelter in danger we learn to dwell there as our abiding home when the danger is past.

II. What God will be to us and do for us.

1. He will deliver us from Satan and from sickness.
2. He will deliver us from fear as well as harm and keep our hearts in perfect rest.
3. He will guard us from all evil by angelic protection and ceaseless providence.
4. He will answer our prayers and honor and bless us.

5. With long life will He satisfy us and show us His salvation.

These are some of the precious promises of this blessed psalm.

III. What He expects of us in order that we may claim His blessing and His healing.

1. That we should abide in Him, dwelling in the secret place of the Most High, and abiding under the shadow of the Almighty. This is the secret of every blessing, fellowship with Christ, intimate union and abiding communion with our Lord.

2. We must confess Him as our Guardian and Deliverer. "I will say of the LORD, 'He is my refuge and my fortress' " (91:2). We must say it as well as feel it. We must commit ourselves openly and unreservedly to His care. And as we do so He will honor our faith and be to us all we take Him for.

3. We must trust Him. We must say, "in whom I trust" (91:2). "Under his wings you will find refuge; his faithfulness will be your shield and [buckler, KJV]" (91:4). The shield is the figure of faith. The buckler represents the sort of faith that is so fastened to us that we cannot lose it, and like the ancient buckler it is part of our very dress and inseparable from us. This is the faith that God gives and that overcomes all things and makes all things possible.

4. We must give up our doubts and fears. This is

not only a promise, but a command. "You will not fear the terror of night" (91:5).

5. We must tread upon the lion and adder. We must take the place of victory. We must put our feet upon the necks of our adversaries. We must treat our spiritual enemies as conquered foes and we must do it in the very beginning, while they are young, before they get the mastery.

6. We must set our love upon Him, choose Him as our supreme object and desire and be wholly consecrated to His will and glory. It is of these He says, "I will rescue him" (91:14). He is proud of our consecration. There is nothing He will not do for the heart that wholly belongs to Him.

Psalm 92

Psalm 92 offers a precious promises of healing. "The righteous will flourish like a palm tree, they will grow like a cedar of Lebanon" (92:12). Here we have both loftiness and strength. We have height and depth—the stature of the palm and the roots of the cedar. You may go through the woods during the spring days and you will see a little vine, the creeper, without any strength in itself, hanging to a great oak. That little creeper is just as strong as the oak. It has not any strength of itself, but has all the strength of the great tree. It is the picture of a weak, helpless disciple leaning on the great, strong Lord. You do not need to be strong, but God is strong, and He gives you His strength.

It goes on to say, "planted in the house of the LORD, they will flourish in the courts of our God. They will still bear fruit in old age, they will stay fresh and green" (92:13–14). Surely, that is a blessed kind of healing, for old age is usually barren; old age ceases to bear fruit. After a certain period almost all sorts of vegetable and animal life cease to produce and bring forth fruit. But like the ivy you can lean upon the giant tree, taking the strength of God.

Psalm 105

Passing over for a moment one or two psalms we come to Psalm 105. Here we find some references to the children of Israel, and God's dealings with them. "He brought out Israel, laden with silver and gold, and from among their tribes no one faltered" (105:37). He brought them forth out of Egypt. He has just been telling us of the death of the firstborn and the leading of the Lord, and this is the way He brought them. He supplied their money, and He supplied their strength because He had promised that He would do it. He had made a covenant at Marah: "If you listen carefully to the voice of the LORD your God and do what is right in his eyes, if you pay attention to his commands and keep all his decrees, I will not bring on you any of the diseases I brought on the Egyptians, for I am the LORD, who heals you" (Exodus 15:26). God kept them strong. Caleb tells that he was as fresh at 85 as a man at 25. And they would all have been kept if they had not disobeyed God.

But God works both ways—the covenant of death and the covenant of life—and so they perished for their disobedience and unbelief.

Psalm 107

And so again in Psalm 107 we have a series of pictures of God's dealings with man. In the 17th verse, "Some became fools through their rebellious ways and suffered affliction because of their iniquities." They have done wrong, and God has no other way to wake them up. "They loathed all food and drew near the gates of death. Then they cried to the LORD in their trouble, and he saved them from their distress" (107:18-19). He is a gracious Lord; He hears their cry. "He sent forth his word and healed them; he rescued them from the grave" (107:20). He did not send a drug or a doctor or a prescription; He sent His Word. "Let them give thanks to the LORD for his unfailing love and his wonderful deeds for men. Let them sacrifice thank offerings and tell of his works with songs of joy" (107:21-22). This is a beautiful picture of God's tender mercy to the poor, troubled sinner.

Psalm 110

Psalm 110 is a psalm for the young as well as the old. "Your troops will be willing on your day of battle. Arrayed in holy majesty, from the womb of the dawn you will receive the dew of your youth" (110:3). It is a picture of Jesus Christ. And the one that is addressed here is Christ, the Son of

Man. The dew of youth means that it is His youth, and He just bedews us with His youth. That is divine healing. It is a little of the life of the Son of God, the freshness that bedews us with His Holy Spirit. "Your troops will be willing [or 'will be a free-will offering'] on your day of battle." Then this will be the result: they will be clothed with the beauty of holiness; They will be fresh from the womb of the dawn and sparkling with the dew of Christ's youth.

Psalm 116

The first nine verses of Psalm 116 are a peculiarly beautiful note of praise.

"I love the LORD, for he heard my voice; he heard my cry for mercy" (116:1). It is not merely "I thank the Lord," but "I love Him because He is so good." Have you ever awakened refreshed and rested after weariness and suffering and said, "I love the Lord because He is so good?" Tell Him you love Him; do not wait until you get to heaven.

Well, what was it; what was the matter? "Because he turned his ear to me, I will call on him as long as I live. The cords of death entangled me, the anguish of the grave came upon me; I was overcome by trouble and sorrow" (116:2-3). You see this is meant for hard cases. It is just framed for people who are in a desperate physical condition. It is the testimony of people who have been dreadfully sick and got well. I have been thinking since I read this over what a beautiful prayer book for the sick these psalms of David would make!

Next he tells us what he did. "Then I called on the name of the LORD: 'O LORD, save me!' " (116:4). He did not lose heart. He did not say what is the use. He just called. He put his whole strength in it and was determined that God should hear him. He called. He put his whole strength in it and called on the name of the Lord. "Ask whatever you wish, and it will be given you" (John 15:7). Do not say, "O Lord, Lord, Lord, why don't You help me?" But say, "O loving Father, O dear Lord, You are so good. O Lord, I beseech You, deliver my life." His life was in danger. He did not have to cry long. He only puts half a verse in his prayer, and all the rest is praise. He says, "The LORD is gracious and righ-teous; our God is full of compassion. The LORD protects the simplehearted; when I was in great need, he saved me" (Psalm 116:5-6). He just knew little enough to expect the Lord to help him.

"Be at rest once more, O my soul, for the LORD has been good to you. For you, O LORD, have delivered my soul from death, my eyes from tears, my feet from stumbling, that I may walk before the LORD in the land of the living" (116:7-9). He is going to live now wholly for God, for He has been so good to him.

Psalm 121

Is there anything better for the home, the business or the journey than Psalm 121, especially the last verses?

He who watches over Israel
  will neither slumber nor sleep.
The LORD watches over you—
  the LORD is your shade at your right
      hand;
the sun will not harm you by day,
  nor the moon by night.

The Lord will keep you from all harm—
  he will watch over your life;
the LORD will watch over your coming and
      going
  both now and forevermore. (121:4-8)

He is our Preserver, our Keeper—keeping our
bodies, keeping our spirits, keeping all our life.

Psalm 127

Is there a sweeter sedative than Psalm 127:2? "In
vain you rise early and stay up late, toiling for food
to eat—for he grants sleep to those he loves." What
is more necessary for health than sleep? What is
harder than to force it, and what is more needful
than rest? What a beautiful verse! "He grants sleep
to those he loves." He puts you in the place of His
beloved before He gives you sleep. You have to be
His beloved first. I dare say that many times when
you have been nervous or weary or worn you have
felt you must just get the love of God before you
could sleep. And He wants to keep you that way.
To His beloved He gives sleep. Take the place of
love and you will find rest and strength.

Psalm 145

We have here some precious promises for the time of physical need. "He fulfills the desires of those who fear him; he hears their cry and saves them. The LORD watches over all who love him, but all the wicked he will destroy" (145:19-20).

Psalm 102

And now we go back to the two psalms that we have passed over, because they are like the 91st, the mountaintops of healing. There are two linked together, the 102nd and the 103rd, for these psalms often go in pairs.

In the 23rd verse of Psalm 102 we read, "In the course of my life he broke my strength; he cut short my days"—sickness, decay, prostration, paralysis, helplessness, complete collapse, inevitable death. Everybody says so. Strength gone. Constitution exhausted. "He broke my strength; he cut short my days." It was evident that his days were numbered. There was no hope. He might as well give up and die. That is the situation. He had quite made up his mind for a while that it was death. Then came the reaction. The breath of hope and prayer, the pitiful plea of helplessness and the prayer for help. And is there anything more pathetic than the prayer of helplessness? Oh, it has often cheered our heart. "So I said: 'Do not take me away, O my God, in the midst of my days; your years go on through all generations'" (102:24).

You cannot fail to see the point. Man's are days, God's are years. With God, he says, a year is as much as a day with me. I have just a little bit of life, Lord. You have all the ages. You have the ages of eternity, Lord. You that are so rich in time, rich in life, let me have my little store. Is it not pathetic? Is it not beautiful? Is it not enough to touch the heart of God Himself? It is like the child that cried, "Save me because I am so little." Get little and then the Lord will save you. Don't try to be big. Don't try to be eloquent. It makes one tired when people say, "I cannot pray well." People that pray well are bores.

Then he says,

> In the beginning you laid the foundation of
> the earth,
> and the heavens are the work of your
> hands.
> They will perish, but you remain;
> they will all wear out like a garment.
> Like clothing you will change them
> and they will be discarded.
> But you remain the same,
> and your years will never end. (102:25-27)

Oh, mighty God; oh, Father of eternity; oh, rich Source and Resource of life, pity Your little child whose life is like a span, and give me just a little more. And God hears the prayer, and the very next word is a burst of praise.

Psalm 103

> Praise the LORD, O my soul;
>   all my inmost being, praise his holy name.
> Praise the LORD, O my soul,
>   and forget not all his benefits—
> who forgives all your sins
>   and heals all your diseases,
> who redeems your life from the pit
>   and crowns you with love and
>   compassion,
> who satisfies your desires with good things
>   so that your youth is renewed like the
>   eagle's. (103:1-5)

This will not mean much to you if you have not actually lived it. Some of you know what it is— the health that is out of weakness made strong, and that lives on the bosom of God.

One is impressed by the completeness of this doxology. It covers everything, all kinds of healing and health. It is the life of God, it is the mercy and salvation of God, "Who forgives all your sins" (103:3). He starts at the right place. There is always need for a fresh touch of grace. Do not try to walk on a plane of independence, but get right down at the foot of the cross. There may be things in your heart that you did not know were there. There may be little films from the very atmosphere of the world, but, oh, it is exquisite to get right down at the feet of Christ and say, "He forgives all." He is so holy that the heavens are unclean before Him. And so, come, sufferer, come to the blood every time and take a fresh cleansing even for what you do not know, and just live under the blood.

And then the healing is complete: He "heals all your diseases" (103:2).

But that is not half of the blessing. When all your diseases are healed you are not half healed. He "redeems your life from the pit" (103:4). You are well today, but tomorrow you would break all your bones if the Lord did not hold you up. You are walking through death all the time and the elements of poison and disease. Why don't you die? Why, the Lord "redeems your life from the pit."

But that is not half yet. He "crowns you with love and compassion" (103:4). That is the sweet nearness that it gives you, the fondness and the oneness of the Father's heart. For when He comes into your body He gets a closer hold of you. I do not know how we would know the love of God if we did not have Him in our very bones. When He is in every throb of the heart, in every bone of the body, He seems nearer to the soul. Do not try to be too stiff and cold, too regular and proper. There is a place for love and emotion, and the happy child and the overflowing hallelujah, and they know it best who are conscious that the Lord is for the body and the body is for the Lord (1 Corinthians 6:13).

But that is not all; the very best is still to come. He "satisfies your desires with good things so that your youth is renewed like the eagle's" (Psalm

103:5). That is divine life that comes after divine healing. That is being lifted to a higher plane and kept there all the time. That is being healed when you are well, as well as when you are sick. It is the overflowing life of God in the human frame and in the human heart. That is the ideal life of this beautiful psalm. These psalms are far beyond the experience of most lives. May God help us to live up to them and then help others to enter in!

CHAPTER 9

The Great Atonement

Surely he took up our infirmities
and carried our sorrows,
yet we considered him stricken by God,
smitten by him, and afflicted. (Isaiah 53:4)

Let us consider some reasons for applying this standard and cardinal passage, in this greatest chapter of the greatest of the prophets, to the subject of divine healing.

Sickness

The first reason here that we may apply this without any doubt as a ground for the Lord's healing is the use of the word "griefs" (KJV) [infirmities, NIV] in this text, "he took up our infirmities." The original word is found about 100 times in the Old Testament. Every time but this it is translated "sickness." This is the only instance where it is translated "griefs." This must be because the translator could not quite understand the sense of using "sickness" here. It might have been on the principle of trying to make the Bible sound more rational that this word was inserted. "Griefs" is not altogether a mistranslation, but the word really means "disease." This verse covers the atonement of Christ for our bodies, the provision of His redemption for these mortal attacks.

Took Up

The next reason for applying this verse in the Bible is the word "borne" (KJV) [took up, NIV]. "He took up our infirmities." This word is also a kind of technical term. It has a theological meaning which is most clearly defined in many of the passages in which we find it. It is applied to the scapegoat that bore away the sins of the people. It is used in this chapter where we are told that He bore the sins of many. It is found in John where we are told that the Lamb of God "takes away the sin of the world" (John 1:29). So it means not mere sympathy or mere relief, but it means substitution, one bearing another's death. Christ literally substituted His body for our body. That is the meaning of the words, "Surely he took up our infirmities" (Isaiah 53:4). He took them upon Himself and relieved us of the load by His atonement.

Christ's Death

The third reason why we apply this passage to divine healing is the use of the word for sickness later in the chapter. In the 10th verse, we are told that it pleased the Lord to make Him sick. "Yet it was the LORD's will to . . . cause him to suffer," or literally, as Dr. Young has translated it, "He hath made Him sick in smiting Him."

We are told by physicians who have explained the causes of the death of Christ that He died from rupture of the heart. He did not die from the ordinary causes incident to crucifixion, but He died from a spasm that caused His heart to burst. When they came to Him He was dead, while the others who were crucified with Him were still alive. He died from the disease which He bore for us. So there is a sense in which Christ was really sick, but it was in our place. It is added, "and by his wounds we are healed" (Isaiah 53:5).

Matthew's Translation

Here is the fourth one. Matthew 8:17 confirms its application to physical healing. "He took up our infirmities and carried our diseases." There you have the literal translation of the word "diseases," and there you have the double use of the verb. Matthew's translation bears out in every part the application of this verse to the healing of the body. Both words, "infirmity" and "diseases," denote physical difficulty and disability. The one may be a lack of strength; the other may be a condition of physical disease. Still further, the use that Matthew makes of the verse makes it quite positive that he was referring to the body alone. He quotes the passage in direct connection with Christ's miracles of healing. "When evening came . . . he . . . healed all the sick" (8:16). The reason that He healed the people was because Isaiah said He would. Now, if Isaiah did not mean healing, this verse would be irrelevant. Isaiah must have meant healing, or Matthew would not have quoted it.

Healed by His Wounds

Once again, to strengthen the argument, we have the opening clause of this great verse, "He was pierced for our transgressions, he was crushed for our iniquities; the punishment that brought us peace was upon him, and by his wounds we are healed" (53:5). Here we have all the different phases of Christ's death. "Pierced for our transgressions," or actual sins.

"Crushed for our iniquities." Iniquities are different from transgressions; they are something in us. It has reference to the state of our heart, to our moral and spiritual condition. What a man is is much worse than what a man does, so Christ died for what you are as well as what you have done.

"The punishment that brought us peace was upon him." That means our spiritual blessing, our new life, our happiness, our peace and rest, our deliverance from the curse of sin and consciousness of it, our union with God in the Holy Spirit. All this was bought for us by His chastisement.

So we have three things in this gospel: transgressions atoned for, our sinful nature laid on Him, our new life bought by Him.

"By his wounds we are healed." That makes the inventory complete. Without that it is only a partial list; with that it is fourfold and entire. But to say "By his wounds we are healed" just means spiritual healing is redundant. He has said that in the previous clause, "He was pierced for our transgressions, he was crushed for our iniquities; the punishment that brought us peace was upon him." It must mean something else—physical redemption through His agony as our substitute.

Now, if you will put those four points together, I do not see how any unprejudiced mind can doubt for a moment that this passage covers the healing of our bodies through the atonement of Christ.

Surely

But, again, we want to notice the force of the word "surely," in this passage. "Surely he took up our infirmities and carried our sorrows." Why did He say "surely"? Why did He say it here? Well, to say the least, it is an underlining of the passage intended to mark it as very important. It makes it not only important, but absolutely true. It is because in the beginning of the chapter he stepped out with diffidence and hesitation, and said, "Who has believed our message?" (Isaiah 53:1). "Lord, they will not believe what I am going to say, and especially when I say anything about the power of the Lord, they will be sure to doubt it. If I talk about historical facts they may believe it, but if I go and tell them about a divine arm that can take hold of man's weaknesses, if I reveal a power that can do great things they will doubt my testimony." "Who has believed our message and to whom has the arm of the LORD been revealed?"

(53:1). Therefore, the Lord just says, "Isaiah, tell them it is true, and put My oath behind it, and say, 'Surely, this particular part of the gospel is true, because it does reveal the arm of the Lord; it does show the power of the Lord.' "

Our Sorrows

But we want to call your attention still further to the other word in this text, "sorrows." "Surely he took up our infirmities and carried our sorrows" (53:4). We have told you that the word "infirmities" means physical disease, sickness of the body. That is the ordinary meaning of the word 99 times out of 100. Here is added another word, "sorrows." I have no doubt that it is a true translation. The only variation that I have seen suggested is the word "pains." It might mean "pains," but I think I like "sorrows" best. It may mean a good many things. It may mean the sensitive, suffering part of sickness. It may mean that which accompanies disease. The worst diseases are often painless, and sometimes the severest pains are connected with the least important diseases, so you can see at once the difference between disease and pain. But, blessed be His name, He covers both. He will not only take away disease, but He will take away the symptoms which accompany it, too. You can bring Him your racking headache just as well as the consumption or the heart disease that is eating away your life.

Again, it may mean mental disease—the ills of the mind—and you know what a large catalog they are, insanity in all its forms. Doubtless it can be healed. God does give many instances of the healing of mental diseases through the name of the Lord Jesus Christ. If you know of any dear friend suffering from this most fearful of all ills, do not hesitate to ask and expect God to help and heal.

But this word "sorrows" has another meaning. Doubtless it means the heartbreak and the inward griefs that affect our feelings and affections and bring an anguish worse than sickness—the burdens of Gethsemane. The more of joy you know, the more of sorrow you will always have. The nearer you get to Him, the oftener will you walk through the gardens of Olivet. But, thank God, He has redeemed you from sorrow. And while pains will hurt, there will come a joy a little sweeter for their hurt. There will come deliverance from their bondage. It is one thing to weep. It is another thing to triumph through your tears and have your sorrow turn to joy. There are people that are crushed with sorrow, and there are people that rise through their trials and their cares. You may rise and triumph through Him. You may go through life with a chastened joy, with a gladness that has in it a touch of gravity, but without a bit of the graveyard. It is yours by the redemption of Jesus Christ.

Carried

Our text is growing bigger and bigger. Why are the two verbs in it? "surely he *took up* our infirmities and *carried* our sorrows." Ah, that is the best of all. It means that He did not only take them when on the cross, and assume them as our Substitute, but it means that He keeps taking them still. And that evermore His hands are reaching out to take them one by one from you and carry them for you in the priesthood of His ascension. "Took up" means on the cross, but He carries them every moment on the throne.

So there are two things. First, you are to believe that He took them once for all. Then there is the putting them over, the laying them on Him, the transferring of every burden as it comes to you. It is living out that beautiful verse, "Do not be anxious about anything, but in everything, by prayer and petition, with thanksgiving, present your requests to God" (Philippians 4:6).

Now you cannot stop being careful for everything just by mere negation, as the folly of Christian Science teaches. That will not do. I cannot say there is nothing the matter with me when there is. I may say there is no trouble. But there is trouble. I cannot cancel my debts by saying there are no debts. But I can hand them over to another. Here is a letter from a friend: "Send your creditors to me. Send your bills to me, call upon me." And you just go to his office and hand them over. And your friend takes them, and you can say, "There is nothing the matter; everything is all right." You can be careful for nothing, but not like a blind Buddhist, or a silly ostrich, who hides his head in the sand and thinks there is no hunter because he cannot see him. "Do not be anxious about anything" is only half the remedy. Listen: "In everything, by prayer and petition, with thanksgiving, present your requests to God." That is the way to hand them over. Give them to Him. Tell Him about them. He that bore them on the cross will carry them day by day, and then the care will disappear because the load is gone.

CHAPTER 10

Divine Healing in Isaiah

We have already referred to that great chapter which is the cornerstone of the gospel, Isaiah 53. And we have seen in it what abundant reason there is to appropriate and apply the great atonement set forth therein to our physical needs. But there are many other passages in this great evangelical prophecy that may be equally applied to the needs of our body and the quickening life of God in our mortal flesh.

The Promise of Strength

"But those who hope in the LORD will renew their strength. They will soar on wings like eagles; they will run and not grow weary, they will walk and not be faint" (Isaiah 40:31).

In the previous verses we are reminded of the fallibility of human strength and the divine sufficiency for those who have no might. Here we learn that they may exchange their weakness for the strength of God by waiting on the Lord. This brings us at once to the heart of the subject. The very essence of the Lord's healing is the imparting of the life of Christ to the human frame by the Holy Spirit. This is obtained by waiting on the Lord. Not the habit of passively waiting until our prayers are answered, but the attitude of receiving from Him in living communion the imparted strength of His own life. Just as the branch draws its life from the vine. Just as the graft attached to the trunk of the tree becomes adjusted to its new sources of supply and draws from the sap its nutriment and life. Just as the dew gathers round the plant and fills the flower cup and refreshes the whole vegetable creation. So the heart can learn to receive from Him who is the Fountain of life, breath by breath, vital energy and physical renewing. This is an exchange of strength. We lay down our strength and receive His instead.

The effect is a great uplift. "They will soar on wings like eagles." This is the first effect of a great blessing. We need these hours of elevation and even if the high altitude is not always maintained, yet it prepares us for the reactions that follow and the quieter plane of daily life. For next we are brought back to the earth again and called to run the race of some supreme exertion, some difficult undertaking, something that requires the putting forth of our utmost energy. And God does give strength for these emergencies, the nights of watching, the days of unremitting toil, the pressure of extreme labor or suffering. But this is not the normal attitude of life.

And so we come to the next stage, "They will

walk and not be 'faint." This is the plod of life. This is the plane of the commonplace. This is where the hardest strain really comes and where the grace and strength of God are most manifest. But it is the long pull that tells and wears. And for this the strength of God is adequate. "Those who hope in the LORD . . . will walk and not be faint."

Yes, there is in Christ physical help for the daily, hourly steppings of duty and toil that will put zest into our labor, spring into our steps and freshness into our spirit. Happy are they who have learned the secret of waiting on the Lord.

Righteousness and Healing

" 'I have seen his ways, but I will heal him; I will guide him and restore comfort to him, creating praise on the lips of the mourners in Israel. Peace, peace, to those far and near,' says the LORD. 'And I will heal them' " (57:18-19).

Here we have the picture of a soul that has gone astray and been suffering under the chastening of the Lord. "I was enraged by his sinful greed; I punished him, and hid my face in anger" (57:17). And the chastening for a time seemed to be in vain. "I was enraged . . . and hid my face in anger, yet he kept on in his willful ways" (57:17). But at last the stubborn will broke and instantly the heart of God flew to meet His returning child. "I have seen his ways, but I will heal him" (57:18). Here we have healing as the result of repentance and returning to God. But this is not all. "I will guide him and restore comfort to him" (57:18).

But there is another healing a little farther on. After the soul has been led into the fullness of Christ and the "peace, peace" of the Spirit's in-breathing, then, for the second time the Lord says, "I will heal them" (57:19). This is different from the first healing. When first we come to God for physical help He meets us on the ground of faith and promise. He doesn't wait for a deep spiritual experience, but blesses us immediately. Our first experience of healing is usually easy and free from the tests and conflicts of our maturer life. But later, after we have entered into all the experiences of these verses, we reach a deeper physical life, one that draws its strength from Christ by the Holy Spirit and finds in Him a new source of health and life. This becomes the habit of faith. It is not mere deliverance from some sudden and special attack of disease, but a normal strength that draws its support continually from Jesus as the Head of our body and the life of all our being.

The Life of Love and the Experience of Healing

"Then your light will break forth like the dawn, and your healing will quickly appear; then your righteousness will go before you, and the glory of the LORD will be your rear guard" (58:8).

"The LORD will guide you always; he will satisfy your needs in a sun-scorched land and will strengthen your frame. You will be like a well-watered garden, like a spring whose waters never fail" (58:11).

Here we have a still deeper experience of life
and healing. It is not mere righteousness now, but
love. The soul has been taught the true fast which
the Lord loves: to undo the heavy burdens, to let
the oppressed go free, to break every yoke, to deal
out bread to the hungry, clothe the naked and
bring the poor and outcast home. "Then [our]
light will break forth like the dawn and [our] healing will quickly appear. . . . [The LORD] will satisfy [our] needs in a sun-scorched land and will
strengthen [our] frame. [We] will be like a well-
watered garden, like a spring whose waters never
fail." Here is the rich and overflowing life of God
springing from a heart full of love and benevolence. Watering others we become watered ourselves. Our health springs. It is not pumped up
from a dry well, but is the overflow of a great arte-
sian fountain. Our very frame is strengthened.

There is something fine in this figure. It reaches
to the marrow. This is not necessarily the fat that
is on our bones, but in our bones. Some people are
made of dry bones. They are parched and pinched
and always seem to be at starvation point. There is
no unction, freshness or heartiness about them.
Their lives are hard and hidebound, like Balzac's
dreadful hero whose skin was too tight for him
and at last squeezed him to death. Others seem to
be always mellow, wholehearted, fresh and overflowing with sympathy, cheer and help for others.
Their bones have been made fat. They have some
marrow in them. This is the life that God gives. It
is a higher kind of health and imparts exhilaration

and spring to every movement and impulse.

So we have found in the book of Isaiah three kinds of health. There is that which comes from waiting on the Lord (40:31). There is that which comes from getting right with God (57:18). And there is that which springs from the overflow of the life of love (58:8, 11). How very significant it is that all these physical blessings spring from spiritual conditions and seem to belong to the very nature of things. A man's health, therefore, is largely a matter of higher conditions. The more we ascend in the spiritual plane the more directly are we in touch with all the sources of divine and supernatural life which center in Christ the Living One and the Fountain of Life to all who abide in Him.

CHAPTER 11

Natural and Supernatural Healing

Until after the time of Solomon there seems to have been no departure from the simplicity of the ancient faith with respect to the body. But he laid the foundation for that departure from God by an alliance with the world which led to all the disasters of his people in the succeeding generations.

Allying himself with Egypt and introducing its luxuries, refinements and intermarriages, there soon followed, no doubt, its physicians too. The grandson of Solomon, King Asa, is the first example of their treatment in the entire Bible. His act is mentioned with manifest disapproval, as indicating distrust in God, and is marked by God's displeasure in its fatal termination. It is marked by a whole series of gradual departures from God through seeking human alliances in his exigencies. "Because you relied on the king of Aram and not on the LORD your God" (2 Chronicles 16:7), was the same principle which a little later caused his death. "Though his disease was severe, even in his illness he did not seek help from the LORD, but only from the physicians" (16:12).

In a published address one speaks of those "who have not sufficient faith in God to see Him in and through the use of means." Then they add, "The use of means ought not to lessen our faith in God. And our faith in God ought not to hinder our using those means which He has given us for the carrying out of His own purposes." It is strange that this distinction is not brought out by the Holy Spirit in this, the first reference to the subject in the Scriptures. Why does the Lord not blame King Asa for not asking a blessing on the physicians? How is it that the forbidden act was not the neglect of this, but seeking the physicians instead of the Lord? His going to them is not regarded as an evidence or an opportunity for faith in God, but the reverse. And is it not the usual rule of human nature to lean harder on the smallest twig of the visible and the human than upon the whole omnipotence of an unseen God? The real test of faith is to be willing to step out on the seeming void and expect to find the Rock beneath.

The case of Naaman, a little later, is a pleasing contrast. His disease was incurable, and especially suggestive of the connection between sickness and sin. His first application was about as far back as the most ignorant and blundering soul could wish for its encouragement. Overflowing with pride and self-consciousness, he came to the prophet's door and expected attention and consideration, but received the deathblow, first to his self-will and then to his sickness. How wisely and bravely the old prophet left him with God, and let him down into the death of self!

So it must ever be. Naaman must die before the leprosy can be cleansed and the healing come. And he dies, as every other must, by an act of faith. And how simple an act! Only implicit obedience to the divine Word. He does just what the prophet tells him, and he does it through to the end. That is faith.

For salvation, for healing, for everything, faith is to do just what God tells us, and then leave the result with Him. Are you sick? There is a command in James (5:14-15) as explicit as Elisha's orders. Simply, promptly, fully obey it, and God will hold Himself as much bound to honor His own word as He does you to obey it.

Naaman's faith had to be continuous, abiding and persistent. He had been commanded to wash seven times in Jordan. This involved the very essence of faith; viz., an act which at first perceives no sign of the answer claimed. Once, twice, three times he entered the sacred river and returned. Once, twice, three times again he repeated it. But there was yet no sign of healing. So must we believe and act and expose ourselves to the humiliation of apparent failure.

How often must it have seemed to him like a vain repetition or foolish play! But he continued until every word had been fulfilled and the order of faith and obedience explicitly, completely carried through. And then the answer came—his flesh "became clean like that of a young boy" (2 Kings 5:14). His leprosy was all gone, and his soul exulting in the consciousness of new and pure and perfect health. So let us believe and wait and finish the steps of faith.

His subsequent history is full of instruction. First, his gratitude prompts him to make a generous return as a thank-offering. And the prophet, with a wise avoidance of even the appearance of mercenary considerations, declines at the time to receive his gift. Next, with a prompt and whole-hearted consecration, he declares his steadfast dedication henceforth to the true God. And then, with a jealous perplexity about his precise duty while attending his royal master in the temples of idolatry, he asks the prophet's counsel. The prophet throws him back on God, and he goes forth to be a witness for God throughout the whole of Syria.

There is one other instance of healing in the later years of the kingdom of Judah. It is the story of Hezekiah. That it was a supernatural and, indeed, a miraculous healing, and not the result of remedies, is evident from the fact that he had been declared by God to be in a dying condition. The distinct statement in Chronicles was that God "answered him and gave him a miraculous sign" (2 Chronicles 32:24) and healed him. If it were miraculous, this disposes at once of the whole question of the means used. They must have been symbolic and not remedial.

His prayer is given with considerable fullness by Isaiah. It began, like many of our prayers, with a wail of unbelief. "I cried like a swift or thrush, I moaned like a mourning dove" (Isaiah 38:14). And many a modern prayer is no better. But at length he reached the point of self-despair with the cry, "I am troubled; O Lord, come to my aid!" (38:14). The deliverance came. "But what can I say? He has spoken to me, and he himself has done this" (38:15).

The faith of Hezekiah in asking a sign was very great. He asked something harder even than his healing. God has given us a still greater sign—the resurrection of Jesus Christ from the dead. After this, nothing is too hard for us to ask or for Him to do.

Hezekiah did not make the most of his new life. He allowed his blessing to lift up his heart in foolish pride, and a greater blow had to come, which left his kingdom and household a heritage of sorrow.

The attempt of some to make the healing of Hezekiah a warrant for the use of medical remedies in our sickness is fatally weak in these respects:

1. He was incurably sick, and no remedy could be a means.
2. His healing was called "miraculous," and if so, could not in any sense be natural.
3. The application used is called a sign. At least this seems to be implied in the last two verses of Isaiah.

4. It was administered by Isaiah through a special divine revelation and not through medical science.

5. There was no resorting to physicians whatever, but from the first a simple waiting upon God.

6. The plaster of figs may have been no more than the anointing with oil in James; viz., a sign that the case had been committed to and undertaken by the Lord.

7. Hezekiah did what he was told by the Lord exactly, and faith should do just what God's Word still teaches us in sickness.

CHAPTER 12

Healing in His Wings

But for you who revere my name, the sun of righteousness will rise with healing in its wings. And you will go out and leap like calves released from the stall. (Malachi 4:2)

This is a vision of the springtime of the ages, with its glorious sunshine and its overflowing life.

The vision came to the last of the Old Testament prophets as he looked out from the severe and cheerless winter of Israel's trials to the brighter future their Messiah was to bring.

Sunrise and Light

The first picture is the sunrise and the light. Another prophet had caught the same vision and had written, three centuries before, "The people walking in darkness have seen a great light; on those living in the land of the shadow of death a light has dawned" (Isaiah 9:2).

Looking across the gulf of four centuries, Malachi saw the rising dawn of the Christian age and the light which was to shine from the face of Jesus Christ on a lost and dark world. It was the vision of a glorious sunrise. How literally our Lord fulfilled the prophecy and claimed the promise as He stood amid the false teachings and perverted light of His age and cried aloud, "I am the light of the world. Whoever follows me will never walk in darkness, but will have the light of life" (John 8:12).

Christ is the sun of righteousness. All other teachers were but light bearers. They shine only with reflected light. But He came as a divine luminary, bearing the direct light of God Himself into the world's darkness. "In the past God spoke to our forefathers through the prophets at many times and in various ways, but in these last days he has spoken to us by his Son" (Hebrews 1:1-2). The teachings and the example of Jesus Christ bring to us the revelation of God's will and His purposes of love and mercy toward our fallen race.

But Christ did not leave us merely with the light of His Word and His pattern of grace. He has also left us His Holy Spirit as the personal agent through whom the light is brought down to our very hearts and made plain to our blindness and ignorance. Not only does He give us light, but also sight. Just as the solar light would be useless to the physical universe were it not for the atmosphere which diffuses it and communicates to our sensitive organs of vision, so the Holy Spirit has been given to take of the things that are Christ's

and reveal them unto us, and make God's light
personal and sufficient for every quickened soul.

The sunrise that Malachi saw was not merely
the dawn of the Christian era and the rising of the
sun of righteousness in the personal ministry of
Jesus Christ. But there is a sunrise just as real and
glorious that comes to every soul which opens its
vision to the light of God. The words become true
to the individual heart that has long been sitting in
darkness:

> Sometimes a light surprises
>   The Christian while he sings;
> It is the Lord who rises
>   With healing in His wings.

This is especially true in connection with the
ministry and experience of divine healing to
which this promise particularly refers. How difficult it is for the natural mind and heart to
grasp this blessed truth and take the Lord for the
body as freely as for spiritual need. Mere teaching cannot bring us to this. There must be a
revelation of Christ by the Spirit as our Almighty Healer.

We may read the most logical arguments. We
may be familiar with all the literature on the subject. But it will all seem dim and distant until the
Sun of righteousness Himself arises with healing
in His wings. Then it is all so plain that we wonder why we ever doubted. And it seems to us that
all the world must fly to His arms if it only knew
what we have come to know of His healing love

and power. Then the Christ of Galilee becomes the Christ of today, a living, bright reality. And the light that reveals Him to our trusting heart brings also the faith that receives Him and turns our pain into praise and our night into day.

Dear suffering one, perhaps you have had light enough from books and teachers. Turn to Him and awake to His power, and it will be true of you, "Then your light will break forth like the dawn, and your healing will quickly appear" (Isaiah 58:8).

The Sun of Righteousness

The light brings also with it the righteousness. We do not only need light, but spiritual life and power. We need to be made right with a divine righteousness. Our spiritual condition is intimately connected with our physical blessing. It was God's ancient covenant with Israel, "If you listen carefully to the voice of the LORD your God and do what is right in his eyes, . . . I will not bring on you any of the diseases I brought on the Egyptians, for I am the LORD, who heals you" (Exodus 15:26). Again, in Ezekiel, the covenant was renewed in his gracious promise, "On the day I cleanse you from all your sins, I will resettle your towns. . . . They will say, 'This land that was laid waste has become like the garden of Eden' " (Ezekiel 36:33, 35). The moral and spiritual transformation brings a new world of material blessings.

Faith must begin with a conscience void of offense, and this is something that all our struggles and efforts can never bring. This is the gift of Jesus Christ. This is that righteousness that looks down from heaven and afterwards springs up from the earth. It is a divine righteousness that comes from the revelation of Jesus Christ. It is as natural and spontaneous as the buds and blossoms that come from the kiss of the sunbeams that look down into their lifeless breasts.

Oh, you who are struggling to be good and holy, when will you learn that man did not make himself at the first and cannot make himself over again? When you cease your struggling and in self-surrender and true helplessness accept "the gift of righteousness" you will "reign in life through the one man, Jesus Christ" (Romans 5:17).

His Healing Wings

The Sun of righteousness will arise with healing in His wings. Doubtless this includes all the ills of humanity and covers Christ's complete redemptive work. But why should we exclude the literal healing which formed so large a part of the Master's earthly ministry? Had we lived in the days of the Messiah, we would have known Him chiefly as a healer and a wonder-working rabbi, who touched the brow of pain and made it whole, and whose presence and command drove away spirits of evil from the human breast and brought the demon-possessed victims of insanity to sit at His feet clothed and in their right minds.

The healing of the body through Jesus Christ was no new thought to the ancient prophets. It had been included in the covenant of Moses. It has been the theme of David's songs and Solomon's proverbs. It had been part of the simple practical faith that took God as their theocratic King for all the life of the nation. It had been a prime feature in the glorious picture which Isaiah gave of the Man of sorrows. And, as we have already shown, it formed a leading part in the actual ministry of the Savior. He passed it on to His disciples when He went away, and they, in turn, bequeathed it to the Christian church down to the latest generations.

God always meant the faith of His people to take real things from Him and make external blessings stepping stones to the higher experiences of the unseen. For if God has not become real to us in the things that are patent to our senses and the observation of all men, how can we be assured that the remoter blessings we are claiming for the future have any solid foundation? But when we see God come into our present life, and become as real as our misery and sin and as the pains and sicknesses He heals, then we know that our faith for the future is not a dream. These things are but the firstfruits of the greater blessings of the ages to come.

The Lord is a God of infinite benevolence and goodness and "in him is no darkness at all" (1 John 1:5). Sickness and pain are as foreign to His nature and beneficent will as sin and death. The original creation He made "very good," and the ravages of disease are wholly due to the presence and power of Satan. Christ has come to destroy the works of the devil, and His blessed gospel includes the healing of our diseases as truly as the forgiveness of our sins. Only a prejudiced and faithless theology could restrict the blessings and rob a suffering world of the touch of His healing wings.

But there are two conditions stated by the language of this beautiful text that are very closely connected with the blessing of healing.

The first is a due sense of God's claims upon our obedience and a spirit of reverence and a humble, holy regard for His authority and will. It is expressed by the phrase, "You who revere my name" (Malachi 4:2). This text gives no encouragement to a profane and fanatical confidence that would dictate to God and claim any temporal blessing regardless of His will. We must first be yielded to that will in complete submission. Only then are we able to stand on the ground of faith and claim our blessing, not merely because we want it, but because He wills it.

Another condition is also expressed by the beautiful phrase, "in its wings" (4:2). It is from close and trustful confidence alone that we can claim His healing. We must get under His very wings and in the bosom of His love before faith can claim its highest victories in our inmost being. This is the secret of many a failure. We are not close enough to His heart. We are not simple and childlike enough in our trust. We have not yet come like little birdlings to nestle under the mother wings of God.

> It is to those that fear His name
>   His healing pow'r the Savior brings;
> Oh, let us hide with contrite hearts
>   Beneath His healing wings.

> It is His wings that heal our pains,
>   And soothe the serpent's poisoned stings;
> Close to His bosom we must press
>   To feel His healing wings.

Springtime

The sunrise brings the springtime. "And you will go out and leap like calves released from the stall" (4:2). This is a beautiful picture of the liberty of the animal world. As the young creatures go forth from the confinement of the winter and leap for joy in the freedom of the fields and the gladness of the spring, the life of Christ in a human body and spirit makes all things new. Even age grows young again in the buoyancy of pulses that beat with the energy of divine life and health.

The ancient picture of it is strikingly beautiful, "His flesh is renewed like a child's; it is restored as in the days of his youth" (Job 33:25). "Who satisfies your desires with good things so that your youth is renewed like the eagle's" (Psalm 103:5). "Those who hope in the LORD will renew their strength. They will soar on wings like eagles; they will run and not grow weary, they will walk and not be faint" (Isaiah 40:31).

Such a life is really the beginning of immortality and resurrection life. It is "the earnest" of the age to come. And it is the privilege of all who will recognize and receive God's blessed gift to lost humanity, the Prince of life, the Lord Jesus, our Living Head and Living Bread. This is the great secret that science has not found, that mythology and poetry have dreamed about and reached after, but that the Bible alone has revealed. It was the secret of the Master's life, and it should be ours. "Just as the living Father sent me and I live because of the Father, so the one who feeds on me will live because of me" (John 6:57).

What a wonder of life and grace is here revealed, a Life sent down from heaven to be the life of the world. No wonder that as Malachi looked down the ages, the shadows seemed to flee away, the night departed, and the sunrise of an everlasting day burst upon his vision.

Oh, you who dwell in darkness and misery, "Arise, shine, for your light has come, and the glory of the LORD rises upon you" (Isaiah 60:1). "The night is nearly over; the day is almost here. So let us put aside the deeds of darkness and put on the armor of light" (Romans 13:12). And then let us go forth in the beauty and brightness of the Bride while the watchers say, "Who is this that appears like the dawn, fair as the moon, bright as the sun, majestic as the stars in procession?" (Song of Songs 6:10).

CHAPTER 13

Paul and Divine Healing

I am torn between the two: I desire to depart and be with Christ, which is better by far; but it is more necessary for you that I remain in the body. Convinced of this, I know that I will remain, and I will continue with all of you for your progress and joy in the faith. (Philippians 1:23-25)

The apostle Paul was not only a pattern of our spiritual life in Christ. He was also a striking example of our right and privilege to receive the life of our Lord Jesus Christ into our mortal frame and to take Him for our physical strength as truly as for our spiritual need.

His life was a marvelous spiritual triumph in the face of unparalleled difficulties, pressures, sufferings and mutilations. He seemed to carry a charmed life. Neither Roman rods nor Roman dungeons, malarial dungeons nor hardships of any kind could hinder him from a single service for his Master. Nothing could shorten his glorious life until all his work was accomplished, and he could say, "I have finished the race, I have kept the faith" (2 Timothy 4:7).

What was the secret of that marvelous physical life? The answer involves the whole doctrine of divine healing and reveals to us its deepest and highest principles.

The Standpoint of Divine Healing

It is good for us to approach every divine truth from the right standpoint. Promises unreservedly true and meant for our enjoyment may be beyond our reach because we are not approaching them from the right direction, and because we are not standing on the true ground of faith. In the verse already quoted, Paul discloses the standpoint from which he was able to trust God for his body. It was because his life was not his own, but so dedicated to Jesus that he could truly say, "For to me, to live is Christ" (Philippians 1:21). It was because he had been delivered from the fear of death so fully that he could honestly say, "For to me . . . to die is gain" (1:21). It was because he did not want to live for his own sake, but only for the sake of his Master, and for the sake of others, that he could say in triumph and confidence, "I know that I will remain, and I will continue with all of you" (1:25).

Paul had so completely renounced his own will in the matter of life or death that he claimed divine health not because it was his will, but because it was his Master's will and for his Master's glory. This is sublimely expressed in his noble words to the elders of Ephesus, "However, I consider my life worth nothing to me, if only I may finish the race and complete the task the Lord Jesus has given me—the task of testifying to the gospel of God's grace" (Acts 20:24). He counted his life dear, but not for himself. It would have been dearer for him to go and be with his blessed Master, but he counted it dear because the Lord needed him, and the Lord's people needed him. It was a sacred trust; therefore; he could take it from his Master without a doubt of fear and go forward into the perils and privations that he knew it involved.

This, friend, is the standpoint of divine healing. This is the ground of faith. This is the only place where we have a right to claim any of God's promises. So long as we want blessings for ourselves they are selfish blessings. But as soon as we relinquish our rights and claims and take everything only for Christ, then we can take anything from God because it is for God we are taking it. Then it is God's interest more than ours to bless us.

This was aptly expressed by a dear old saint, who used to say when he got into any trouble, "Oh, Lord, your property is in danger! Oh, Lord, take care of your property." He was so wholly the Lord's that he could honestly feel in looking after himself he was looking after the Lord's property. All things are ours when we are Christ's. So God help us and bring us to the point where we let go even of life itself, as a personal desire, and then take it back as God's will and God's choice, and for God's service and glory. It is the old story of Moriah. It is Isaac laid down and then given back as God's Isaac and no longer as ours. We gain by losing, we lose by holding. The surrendered life is the only safe life. Letting go is twice possessing.

The Secret of Divine Healing

He had a secret. It was a very definite one. It expressed the philosophy of his experience. It was exactly the same secret that he had for his spiritual life. "I no longer live, but Christ lives in me" (Galatians 2:20).

Paul had no sanctification of his own, but it was all summed up in the indwelling life of Christ. And so Paul claimed no physical strength of his own. He had learned the secret of resting in the physical life of his Master, and living upon the supernatural vitality he received from Christ—"renewed day by day" (2 Corinthians 4:16).

He said, "We always carry around in our body the death of Jesus, so that the life of Jesus may also be revealed in our body. For we who are alive are always being given over to death for Jesus' sake, so that his life may be revealed in our mortal body" (4:10-11).

We find a little expression repeated twice [in KJV] here, "The life also of Jesus." Paul had two lives. He had his own life which was mortal and frail and which was always ready to die. But he had another life, "the life also of Jesus." And when his own physical strength gave way, then the life of Jesus came to his aid and carried him through. In other words, he had residing in him the very Person of his blessed Master. Christ's supernatural life sustained Paul's vital energy. When ready to sink, exhausted and all his powers had failed, there came to Paul directly from Christ, through the Holy Spirit, a quickening influence reviving and restoring him and sufficient for all his needs.

Now, we may not understand this. We cannot understand it unless we know the secret too. It is like a telegraphic message in code. We must have the key to the cipher to make any meaning out of it. And the key to this experience is the personal knowledge of the Lord Jesus Christ in your own being. Let us, at least, believe it.

We will find it confirmed by the whole story of his life. Let us recall an incident. In the 14th chapter of Acts, after Paul had preached the gospel at Lystra to a heathen audience with wonderful power, the jealous Jews from Iconium and Antioch came and set the people against him. They incited a cruel riot and persuaded the mob to attack Paul and drag him through the streets of the city and stone him until they left him for dead. We may be quite sure that when Paul's Jewish enemies got a chance to kill him, they did not stop halfway. So far as they could see, Paul was dead. Having been dragged along the hard pavement and left buried amid a heap of stones, to all intents and purposes the life of Paul must have been ready to go out. But it was just then that "the life also of Jesus" asserted itself. And so we read, with great simplicity but with sublime eloquence, "But after the disciples had gathered around him, he got up and went back into the city. The next day he and Barnabas left for Derbe. They preached the good news in that city and won a large number of disciples. Then they returned to Lystra, Iconium and Antioch" (Acts 14:20-21).

Here we see the power of Christ revealed in the hour of utter despair. As his brethren stand around him in loving prayer the Holy Spirit arouses his sinking life, and Jesus touches him with His own physical and endless life. The life of Christ quickens his mortal body, and he springs to his feet and goes on to his work. The next day we find him, not in a hospital, nor on a long vacation, but preaching the gospel. Eventually he goes back to the very place where he had been maltreated and almost killed, and goes on quietly, triumphantly with his work, taking his healing for granted as though it were just the thing to be expected.

So again, we find him at another point in his history telling them of the trouble that came to them in Asia, that

> We were under great pressure, far beyond our ability to endure, so that we despaired even of life. Indeed, in our hearts we felt the sentence of death. But this happened that we might not rely on ourselves but on God, who raises the dead. He has delivered us from such a deadly peril, and he will deliver

us. On him we have set our hope that he will continue to deliver us. (2 Corinthians 1:8-10)

Here is a very clear case of experience. In the first place Paul was sick unto death and de- spaired even of life, when he looked at himself. And it would seem that when he looked at God, the answer was death. Paul's life was not equal to it. He was pressed above measure and above strength. Yet there was another life, the life of his risen Lord, the strength of "God, who raises the dead," on which he depended. And from his own sinking life, Paul looked up to the endless life of Jesus and claimed it in all its resurrection power till he could send back the triumphant shout, "He has delivered. . . . He will deliver . . . He will continue to deliver."

This is the secret of divine healing. It is union with One who is our physical Head as well as the source of our spiritual life. It is to be in touch with the Son of Man who is risen from the dead, in the power of an endless life, and who is the Head of our body and has taught us to understand that "we are members of his body, of his flesh, and of his bones" (Ephesians 5:30, KJV). Paul tells us in another place that our "bodies are members of Christ" (1 Corinthians 6:15). "The body . . . is for the Lord, and the Lord for the body" (6:13). Why should not we understand and claim the secret too?

It does not mean immortality, or life that never can die. But it does mean participation in the life of our risen Lord in such a measure as will make us equal to every duty, every labor and every pressure, until our life-work will be done, and the Master will either call us to Himself or come to meet us. Friend, have you learned the secret "the life also of Jesus"?

The Principles of Paul's Secret

In the first place it did not presuppose that Paul should be strong in his own constitutional strength. On the contrary it was based upon Paul's weakness and was quite consistent with a condition on his part of personal insufficiency. There is every reason to believe that Paul was naturally feeble rather than robust, and that his constant exposures, hardships, and sufferings had had their natural effect in reducing him many times to the very verge of prostration, and even death. And so we find him speaking of the infirmity of his flesh. We find him saying, "We who are alive are always being given over to death for Jesus' sake." "We always carry around in our body the death of Jesus" (2 Corinthians 4:11, 10).

But this did not hinder his taking the strength of the Lord Jesus and being enabled thereby for all that the Master required of him. His health and strength were a divine paradox. "When I am weak, then I am strong" (12:10), he could most truly say. In himself he was physically weak but in reliance upon the physical strength of an indwelling Lord, he was stronger than himself. He was better equipped for his work than even perfect health could have made him.

Here lies the deep secret of divine healing and the explanation of Paul's singular experience recorded in the 12th chapter of Second Corinthians. The "thorn in the flesh" was not removed, whatever that thorn was, but more strength was given than if it had been removed. Therefore, if it was a spiritual trial it was not taken away but double grace was added. And if it was a physical weakness it was not withdrawn but double physical strength was supplied, so that Paul was even stronger than if he had been delivered from this particular trouble.

He could say, "I will boast all the more gladly about my weaknesses, so that Christ's power may rest on me" (12:9). Paul's health was divine strength given in human weakness so he could say, "Though the outward man is perishing, the natural and physical constitution may seem to decay, yet the inward man, the divine life, by Christ's strength is renewed day by day."

In the second place Paul's experience of divine health was not incompatible with the greatest pressures, the severest hardships, the most perilous exposures and the most uncongenial and unfavorable surroundings. Much of his life was spent in damp, unhealthy dungeons. He was often exposed to cold, inclemency, fasting and sleeplessness. A night and a day was he adrift at sea. He was often shipwrecked; again and again he was stoned, beaten with the Roman rods that bruised and lacerated both flesh and bone almost to mutilation. Never did a human body sustain such unspeakable pressures. And yet he went through them triumphantly, always ready for whatever service the Master had for him. "We are hard pressed on every side," he could say, "but not crushed; perplexed, but not in despair; persecuted, but not abandoned; struck down, but not destroyed" (4:8-9). The severest pressures only served to render the more marked the glory and strength of his Lord. He could say, "We have this treasure in jars of clay to show that this all-surpassing power is from God and not from us" (4:7).

In the third place Paul's physical strength was sustained by continual dependence on the Lord Jesus and a life of abiding in Him for physical as well as spiritual life. He gives us the secret in Second Corinthians 4:16 and 18: "Therefore we do not lose heart. Though outwardly we are wasting away, yet inwardly we are being renewed day by day. . . . We fix our eyes not on what is seen, but on what is unseen."

The renewing was "day by day" and only while he looked to the unseen sources of his strength. He did not receive one tremendous miracle which carried him through life. He had learned what Jesus had so fully unfolded in the sixth chapter of the gospel of John in regard to His own life, "Just as the living Father sent me and I live because of the Father, so the one who feeds on me will live because of me" (6:57). Feeding upon Christ, Paul lived by Him. Paul could truly say in the language which he employed elsewhere and in another connection, "In him we live and move and have our being" (Acts 17:28).

We must learn moment by moment to live upon His life. And, while outward pressure increases and personal strength diminishes, we must take a stronger hold upon His everlasting strength. As we wait on the Lord, we must renew our strength until we will "soar on wings like eagles; . . . run and not grow weary, . . . walk and not be faint" (Isaiah 40:31). This was the physical life of Paul. This is the privilege of every believing and obedient child of God.

CHAPTER 14

Questions and Answers

Many practical questions arise in the minds of inquirers concerning divine healing both as respects the doctrine and the personal appropriation. Some of these I will endeavor to answer.

1. In what sense can Christ be said to atone for sickness, when disease involves no such moral element as sin does?

If I owe a debt to a man, not only am I liable, my house is liable, too, and it may be held until my debt is paid. So my body is my house, and it is liable for the debt of my soul to God, even if it has not sinned, as the soul has. Disease is sin's mortgage against my house. But, if the debt is paid, the mortgage is discharged, and my house is free. So Christ has paid my debt of sin and released my body. Judgment has no claims upon it. On the cross of Calvary He bore in His body all my physical liabilities for sin, and therefore He is said to have borne our sicknesses and carried our pains, and by His stripes we are healed.

2. If Christ has provided for the complete removal of our diseases, why should we ever die?

He has not provided that there will be no disease, but that disease, if it comes, will be overcome. Likewise He has not provided that there will be no death, but that should death come, it will be overcome by the glorious resurrection. If there were no death there could be no resurrection. Physical immortality in our human and earthly state would be far less than the glorious and immortal life we will have through our second Adam, in our resurrection life.

3. Why then can't the dead be raised now as in the days of Christ and His apostles?

There is nothing to render such an occurrence impossible, but there is at the same time no scriptural authority to justify our claiming it. The command to exercise this ministry was given to the 12 apostles, not to the 70. And the time for the resurrection of Christ's people is distinctly stated thus: "then, when he comes, those who belong to him [will be made alive]" (1 Corinthians 15:23, 22).

4. If we should always claim healing, however, would it not follow that we should never die?

Not necessarily. There is no need that we should die of disease. The system might just wear out and pass away as naturally as the apple ripens and falls in autumn, or the wheat matures and dies in June. It has simply fulfilled its natural period.

"You will come to the grave in full vigor, like

sheaves gathered in season" (Job 5:26). This is very different from the apple falling in June, with a worm in it. That is disease. The promise of healing is not physical immortality, but health until our life work is done. "With long life will I satisfy him" (Psalm 91:16). We may not all live to the age of 80, but we may all be satisfied. And if we knew that our life would close tomorrow, we should claim strength and sufficiency today.

5. Are we not taught in the Scriptures that submission to God's will is the highest act of faith and obedience?

Yes, and before claiming anything of God we must be in the attitude of profound submission and prostration. But, being in this attitude, we will be led to make very sure that what we submit to is indeed God's will. And we will find that that will does not lay upon an obedient and surrendered child a needless burden of sickness and pain. Rather it desires and demands for us, even more than we can desire it, the help and deliverance Christ has purchased by His blood for our bodies as well as our souls.

6. How may I know His will in any particular case?

We can only know His will from His Word and Spirit. We must not expect a special revelation from His Spirit where His Word has clearly spoken. He has told us clearly in His Word that Jesus has purchased for us redemption for body as well as soul. He has said of one sufferer who represented many more, "should not this woman . . . be set free . . . from what bound her?" (Luke 13:16). He has shown us His father's will by His whole earthly example and acts as well as words, and never in a single case did He decline to help those who trusted Him. Unless He has shown us something different for us so clearly that we cannot question it, we should not question it, but should go forward on these clear encouragements of His Word and take Him at that Word for all.

7. Is not sickness a divine chastening, and really designed for our good, and ought it not so to be received by us?

If we honestly so regard it, why, of course, we should bow under it at the Father's feet, and leave ourselves wholly in His hands. But it is a little inconsistent to say this and then run for the nearest doctor and use every expedient and resource of human skill to get rid of this gracious chastening, and get out of the divine hands. Persons who act so, really believe in their heart that sickness is an evil and that they are perfectly justified in using every legitimate means to remove it. Even if it is a divine chastening, surely prayer is a much more reverent and childlike remedy than medicine.

But, seriously, the whole subject of divine chastening is greatly mystified by those who reason in this way.

God has told us that His chastenings are not random or capricious blows struck without reference to any principle of moral government,

and leaving us wholly in the dark as to their purpose and remedy. God chastens like a father, intelligently and tenderly. He is willing to make us
know His meaning, and how we may escape His
rod. He has told us distinctly that sickness and
suffering are sent when we will not heed His
gentle voice. Even then, if we will listen, repent,
acknowledge our error, learn our lesson and
obey His will the trial will be arrested or removed, and we restored to His love and favor.
The 33rd chapter of Job gives a picture of His
dealings with His children through trial. And
there is no dark, terrific mystery, but the simple,
righteous principle, so clearly laid down in the
New Testament, "If we judged ourselves, we
would not come under judgment. When we are
judged by the Lord, we are being disciplined so
that we will not be condemned with the world"
(1 Corinthians 11:31-32). Even if sickness is a divine chastening, its remedy is to have recourse
to God and, putting ourselves right with Him,
claim His gracious deliverance.

*8. How can I be sure that it is not best for me to be sick
to keep me humble and near to God?*

Well, friend, if the blood of Jesus and the grace
of God and the power of the Holy Spirit are not
sufficient to keep you humble and holy, I do not
see how sickness is going to, unless sickness is a
greater Savior than Christ. And I do not see how
God is going to keep the saints and angels pure in
a world where there will be no pain forever.

9. But don't many people greatly glorify God in their sicknesses and trials? Isn't it a great opportunity for service and testimony?

A true disciple will glorify God anywhere. But how do you know how much more these persons would glorify God, after having shown the spirit of patience and meekness in trial, by rising up in His strength and showing His power to heal, and then going out to witness and work for Him?

How many there are, on the contrary, who wither and fail under the long and crushing weight of years of pain, and become depressed, morbid, and blighted by the furnace. If God wants us well He will not perfectly bless us in sickness. He will sustain us, but He will also prompt us to claim something higher and better.

10. But how do I know that if I were healed I would really use my strength for the glory of God, and not perhaps, like Hezekiah, fail to render according to the benefit received?

The same grace and power that heal the body are also promised to sanctify and keep the soul and may be claimed by the same faith. The first promise is Jehovah Tsidkenu; the second, Jehovah Rophi. Both are equally free, and both must be taken together if our blessing is to be complete.

11. Was not the answer of God to Paul, when he prayed for the removal of his thorn, a lesson to us to accept our trials and sicknesses as God's will and receive more grace to bear them?

Well, in the first place, Paul certainly prayed until he got an answer from heaven, and so we should claim deliverance at the very least until we get a refusal as clear and divine as he did.

In the next place Paul's revelations required a special discipline to counteract the effect of his stupendous revelations. And when we get where he had been we may claim some right to his thorn.

In the third place, if the ordinary doctrine of our opponents is true, that sickness is not from Satan but from God, this could not have been disease, for it was a messenger of Satan.

In the fourth place, there is every reason to believe that it was not sickness, but some humiliating and annoying trial, something that buffeted him rather than incapacitated him, for all through it the power of Christ rested upon him. He does not seem to have been hindered a single day from his ministry, and he adds that "The things that mark an apostle—signs, wonders and miracles—were done among you with great perseverance" (2 Corinthians 12:12).

And finally, we have elsewhere several distinct accounts of his healing from disease, showing that he had anything but a doubtful experience of the efficacy of prayer for his bodily need. In Acts 14:20, we see him by faith rising up from a state of apparent death after having been stoned and dragged through the streets as dead, and immediately going forth to preach the gospel. In Second Corinthians 1:8-11, we see him give up, humanly speaking, to die, through the pressure of a trouble under which he "despaired even of life," and yet was delivered through faith in God who raises the dead.

And in Second Corinthians 4:8-11, we see him often exposed to death and ready to sink, naturally, but finding his weakness a greater occasion for the life of Christ to be manifested in his mortal flesh. Such a man is rather an unfortunate argument to use against divine healing.

12. Why haven't the great and good men of the past and present accepted this doctrine, if it is in the Word of God?

Well, why have they not accepted the doctrine of the Lord's personal coming, the doctrine of baptism, the doctrine of holiness in this life? Simply because the faith once delivered to the saints was lost during the Middle Ages and only partly recovered by Luther, and since then is slowly being restored to the Church of God. We will never have much hold upon divine truth until we take it as God's word, without waiting for the endorsement of human names. But it would not be hard to show a long list of noble names, including Irenaeus, Tertullian, Origen and Justinian among the fathers, the Waldenses and Covenanters in later times, and even Luther, Peden, Cameron, Wesley and Whitfield since the Reformation, who bear witness to the marvelous healing power of God in this way.

13. Why was Epaphroditus "ill, and almost died" (Philippians 2:27)?

I suppose as Paul states because of his extreme self-sacrificing efforts for him. And, perhaps, we might add, to give an opportunity and show the power and grace of God in his healing, for "God had mercy on him" (2:27) and healed him. And I cannot see how his case is anything but an example of God's love and power in healing.

14. Why did Paul leave Trophimus at Miletum, sick?

Well, we do not claim that Paul had any power to heal Trophimus, or that anybody has such power now. It was a matter between Trophimus and his God. Perhaps God had some lesson for him that he had not learned, and therefore, he could not at once be healed. Are there not such cases today, by the hundreds? Didn't God have to leave Job on his back until he learned his heart-searching lesson? And then He healed him immediately.

Divine healing fully recognizes the sovereignty of God, and the state and spiritual attitude of the individual. The case of Trophimus, therefore, is fully in harmony with all its principles.

15. Why is it that many persons who were anointed for healing, and claimed to have been healed, and seemed to have real faith, have died?

We never can read the heart. God only knows if there was a real faith. Many excellent and eminent Christians are found without such a faith. Many who once claimed healing with a victorious faith at a later period are found to be without it and acknowledge it themselves.

There may be various causes for it. Sometimes it is a subtle, spiritual decline in vigorous, energetic fellowship with God. The soul reposing on its pillow of privileges has become at ease in Zion, and lost the edge of its first love. Sometimes a marvelous healing has led it so to rest in what God has done as to let go abiding communion for continued life and power. Sometimes a subtle pride, or lack of love crept in and weakened the spiritual vigor. Sometimes in those who are not healed there is an expectation and hope rather than an immediate and present tense faith. Real faith takes and acts now. Many drift slowly over, expecting to be healed someday, expecting rather than accepting. In many such cases it has been made very plain afterwards that there was no real taking of Christ for strength and healing.

Sometimes the Master is taking home His child. Will He not, in such cases, lift the veil and show the trusting heart that its service is done? How often He does! Dorothea Trudel[1] could not, would not, ask for life. She was going home.

A dear young girl in Michigan who for some time claimed healing, awoke one day from sleep, her face covered with the reflection of heaven. She told her loved ones that the Master had led her to trust for life thus far, but now was taking her to Himself. It is well, and let no one dare to reproach such a heart with unfaithfulness.

16. Why did President Garfield[2] die, in spite of the prayers of the whole nation, including many godly and believing persons?

There was no sort of compliance in this case with the scriptural conditions of answered prayer. He was under the care of a number of earthly physicians, there was no submission of the case directly to God in the ordinance of anointing and the prayer of faith, and, indeed, such a suggestion was, we believe, refused and would be probably in any similar case. Nor was there any evidence of personal faith in God, on his own part, for healing.

In no sense did it come under the scriptural requirements for divine healing, and besides, it is very probable that God was dealing with this whole nation in a public manner through its head, and calling it to repentance without which, not even Noah, Daniel and Job could together have obtained deliverance.

17. Does not James say, "The prayer offered in faith will make the sick person well; the Lord will raise him up. If he has sinned, he will be forgiven" (5:15)?

Yes, all true, and they are forgiven, but it is not a question of forgiveness merely, but of discipline. James also says, in the same passage: "See how the farmer waits for the land to yield its valuable crop and how patient he is for the autumn and spring rains. You too, be patient and stand firm, because the Lord's coming is near. . . . You have heard of Job's perseverance and have seen what the Lord finally brought about. The Lord is full of compassion and mercy" (5:7-8, 11). This is the spirit of the faith that claims and receives divine healing.

18.   But doesn't James speak of the prayer of faith as if it was the faith of the elders that brought the healing?

Happily, the Holy Spirit has anticipated this objection by the first verses in James. He says about this very question of prayer, "When he asks, he must believe and not doubt. . . . That man should not think he will receive anything from the Lord" (1:6-7).

God is not going to make one man's faith a shelter for another's unbelief. He is not going to let us keep our doubts and get our healing. He cares for us too well to let us remain on any lower plane than that of implicit confidence in Him. True, He does give and bless the ministry of prayer for others and enables us to believe for their help. But it is only when they also are right with God and exercising faith for themselves. Then their faith and ours are in one accord and it is really a united prayer. But when we are leaning on another's faith and not looking directly to God ourselves, there is no unity and there can be no power.

19.   Are there not in the New Testament distinct promises of special gifts, power of healing and miracles spoken of in connection with the enduement of the Spirit? And may we not expect these to be exercised by special individuals?

Yes, there are spiritual gifts, but they are never

apart from the Giver. They are not powers possessed by the individual, but the power of the Holy Spirit personally, working through him. "All these are the work of one and the same Spirit, and he gives them to each one, just as he determines" (1 Corinthians 12:11).

No man can claim that he is a healer or a power, or anything but a helpless instrument whom God may be pleased to use in a given case, and will use in so far as the conditions are in accordance with His will. But God will not allow him to do anything differently from what God Himself would do, if you came to Him directly. Now, if you come to God with a heart of unbelief and dependence upon man, you will get nothing. Nor will you if you thus come to His most chosen instruments.

Take, for example, the gift of power for winning souls. This is a real ministry and power. But it gives no power to us to save the sinner apart from his own direct repentance and faith. It is simply the power to lead him to God, and when he comes with a true heart to claim for him acceptance and salvation, and really receive with and for him the blessing and seal of heaven.

So, precisely, in the ministry of healing, the part of the instrument is to lead the sufferer to know the will and Word of God, to trust Him for himself, and then when he truly and trustingly comes, to claim with and for him the blessing promised, and the seal and earnest of the Holy Spirit.

A young lad fell overboard from a ship's deck,

and one of the sailors stood quietly looking at his struggles, while the mother cried frantically, "Why don't you save my boy?" Still he stood until he sank and rose the second time. Then he sprang in and rescued him. "Why did you wait so long?" asked the anxious mother. "I waited till he was too weak to clutch me. Had he done so, we would both have sunk together." Keep your hands off all men if you would really trust God, and then even men can doubly help you.

20. Is there then any need for the ministry of others at all?

Yes, God has appointed the ministry of prayer and given a special promise where two of us are agreed as touching anything we will ask. He has also appointed the ordinance of anointing as the special seal and acknowledgment of His covenant of healing, and our claim. These are divine means, and channels of blessing when received in the spirit of faith in Himself. Their willful neglect would show a spirit of disobedience and self-will, unbecoming the humble disciple.

21. What is the special significance of anointing, and how often should it be administered?

It is an Old Testament symbol of the Holy Spirit. It signifies His personal coming into the body of the person anointed to communicate the healing life and power of Jesus Christ. It sustains to the matter of healing a similar relation to that held by baptism and the Lord's supper in connection with our professions of Christ as a Savior, and our deeper communion with Him spiritually.

It should not be repeated needlessly or with an idea of any potency in itself. If there be any new physical need, or even a new spiritual state enabling us to take hold of Christ for healing in a more effectual manner than before, it may be repeated. But it ought not to be lightly done, or done in any way which could discount or reckon as null and void our former anointing.

22. Why has God made all the remedies we find in nature if He does not intend us to use them?

Perhaps He did not make them any more than He made beer or whiskey. God made the barley and man made the alcohol.

And yet there is in the human body and the natural world a certain *vis medicatrix natura*, as the doctors call it—that is a certain restorative power which is part of His divine beneficence for a world which He foresaw would be cursed with sin and sorrow. And we do not deny that natural remedies may go a certain length and possess a limited value in relieving and healing the body. But:

1. They are limited and extremely uncertain.
2. They are not His way for His children.
3. They are not to be combined in the Scriptures with divine healing.
   a They work through natural, this through supernatural channels.
   b. They do not act on the same principles.

The one is local and specific treatment, the other is a direct vital touch upon the springs of life.

c. All Christ's redemption purchases must be free gifts, by grace without works. So if divine healing is through Christ's blood, it must be a gift of grace alone. We cannot mix our works with it any more than our justification.

d. He must have all the glory. If man touches it, he will be sure to claim it.

e. Faith, by its very nature, is always weakened by a mixture of man's works. If it has a human twig to lean on, it will lean harder on it than on God's mightiest words. It must, therefore, have God only.

To combine the omnipotence of Jesus with a dose of mercury is like trying to go upstairs by the elevator and the stairs at the same moment, or harnessing an ox with a locomotive.

23. *But can't we ask God to bless the means?*

Yes, but that is not divine healing through the name of Jesus alone, as He has prescribed. That is Esau's blessing. There is a blessing even for Esau; but give me Jacob's.

24. *But didn't God prescribe figs for Hezekiah?*

Yes, and if He had prescribed figs for us, we should use them. Hezekiah did just what he was told, and God healed him. We are told to pray,

"[Anointing] him with oil in the name of the Lord" (James 5:14). If we really believe God, we will exactly obey.

The figs did not and could not heal Hezekiah. His case was wholly incurable. They were simply a token that God had the case in hand. They were given at the command of the prophet, and not the physician, who seems to have had nothing whatever to do with this case.

25. Why did Christ use clay?

No doubt for a similar reason, as a token that He was touching this man's disease. But the clay did not heal him. It was the water of Siloam, the type of the Sent One, that washed away both the clay and the blindness, too.

26. Wasn't Luke called the Beloved Physician?

Yes. He had been a physician, but he became an evangelist. Even if he practiced after his conversion, it was no reproach, nor sin. But if God had wanted to guard us against the fanaticism of divine healing, how easy it would have been for Him to record a single instance in which the early believers sent for Luke. He could not have much medical practice in such a wandering life as he led with Paul. The only time we read of the two meeting at the side of a patient, was when Eutychus was killed. And then it is Paul, and not Luke, who seems to have been sent for, and who certainly was used of God to raise him from the dead. Luke himself, who writes the narrative, does not even use a medical term in describing it.

27.   But didn't Paul himself prescribe medicine to Timothy in telling him to take wine for weak digestion?

Well, if this was fermented wine, we must abandon the argument for temperance. If, then, it was unfermented wine, it was simply a diet, and not a drug, and used just as we would suggest tea or chicken soup to a friend. God's Word does prescribe to us all varieties of simple, wholesome food, but not medicine. From Genesis to Revelation you will find no single explicit direction to use human remedies. But you will find numerous directions to bring your sickness to God.

28.   How should I act if I should break my arm?

Ask the Lord to keep it from breaking. Then do not calculate on breaking it, or you may according to your faith. If you should meet someone who has a broken arm, tell him not to try any experiments on God. If they can trust Him, without doubt He will heal anything. But if they cannot surely do so or have any question about it, let them go to the nearest and best surgeon.

For yourself, trust God in the present moment, and do not have any supposes, else you may have Job's experience, "What I feared has come upon me" (Job 3:25).

29.   How should we act in reference to the sickness of others?

First lead them to get right spiritually and learn

the lesson God may have. Then tell them of the great Physician and pray for right conviction and appropriating faith. But do not commit your faith further than they are ready to go of themselves, unless you are specially led of God to do so. Above all, do not allow them to lean upon your faith for their healing. If they can really believe and act in faith, then take hold for and with them with all your heart. When two of you are really agreed in spirit and faith, it will be done.

30. What should we do in the case of children?

If they are our own children, we may act for them. Also if they are substantially laid upon us by the Lord, so that we are responsible for them, we may act for them. But we cannot believe for the children of others where God is looking to someone else to assume this responsibility, as, for example, an unbelieving parent. In the case of the children of others we should be most careful in assuming responsibility. In the case of the children of our orphanage, we would not feel justified in taking this responsibility, in view of the law of the state requiring the care of an attendant physician.

In the case of our own children we may and should teach them to unite with us themselves in faith. We will find it very easy to get their simple hearts to trust Jesus fully.

In all cases of sickness in others where there is danger involved and you have the responsibility, to meet the obligations of the law, it is a great matter, if possible, to have some regular physician who believes in divine healing within call, so as to be responsible if necessary.

31. If we are not immediately conscious of actual healing, after anointing, how should we act?

Keep your eyes off your symptoms and on Christ. He is your life. Your body must be reckoned as good as dead, and He depended upon for strength, moment by moment. Therefore look to Him, draw your strength from Him and be not discouraged at any testing or seeming delay. In nature the root may be cut, and yet the tree only wither after many weeks. The seed may be planted in September, and the winter snows and storms pass over it before the spring and summer bloom and harvest. "See how the farmer waits for the land to yield its valuable crop and how patient he is for the autumn and spring rains. You too, be patient and stand firm, because the Lord's coming is near" (James 5:7-8).

32. How can I consider and call myself healed when there is no sign of it in my body?

How can I go away from the telegraph office and be at rest about the telegram I have just sent, when I see no trace of it as it goes flashing along the wires? If I can trust a telegraph operator, can I not trust my God? Faith must always first call the things that are not as though they were (Hebrews 11), and against hope believe in hope (Romans 4:18). Abraham's faith believed "His body as good as dead" (4:19). More literally, "Without weakening in his faith, he faced the fact that his body was as good as dead . . . Yet he did not waver through unbelief regarding the promise of God, but was strengthened in his faith and gave glory to God, being fully persuaded that God had power to do what he had promised" (4:19-21).

The healing is not in our own body at first—we consider it as good as dead—but in Christ's body. As we look to it, its strength keeps coming into ours. Our "weakness [will turn] to strength" (Hebrews 11:34).

33. But have we a right to call that real which is not real?

If God calls it so, we can echo His declaration. Faith always must first reckon and then receive. When we go to the post office to collect our orders, we must send in our signed receipt before we get any money. So faith must ever send its receipt to heaven before it grasps its answer. And if we have not the faith to do this for divine healing, perhaps we have not the faith for anything.

34. How can I obtain and exercise true and effectual faith for divine healing?

Only by having divine faith as well as divine healing. Only by counting your faith and yourself dead and insufficient, and receiving Christ for this wholly, throwing yourself upon Him for it absolutely. You must claim a faith as perfect as one that believes it has the thing which it has asked, and so has whatsoever it says.

35. *Is all sickness from the devil?*

Sickness may arise from several causes. First, it is sometimes God's chastening. While the devil is the instrument used, God is speaking, and we must hear and repent and learn His lesson. Secondly, it is sometimes Satan's tormenting attack when we are walking in obedience and service. He has power even to simulate all symptoms. He often attacks us after we have given a testimony against him, especially respecting healing, and at other times when in God's special service. At such times we must resist him, and he will flee from us. We must not fear him. Especially we must lay him over on Christ, and He will conquer. But to know it is Satan is half the battle.

Notes

1. Dorothea Trudel was a German woman, renowned for piety and for her success in praying for the sick. At the close of her own life she felt that God's time had come for her homegoing, and refused prayer for herself.

2. James A. Garfield, twentieth president of the United States, was fatally wounded in 1881 by an assassin's bullet. He was an earnest Christian, and nationwide prayer was offered for his recovery.]

SCRIPTURE INDEX